The Silence of Bartleby

Other books by Dan McCall:

Triphammer
Queen of Hearts
Bluebird Canyon
Beecher
Jack The Bear
The Man Says Yes
The Example of Richard Wright

DAN McCALL

The Silence of BARTLEBY

Cornell University Press

ITHACA AND LONDON

First published 1989 by Cornell University Press.

International Standard Book Number (cloth) 0-8014-2320-1
International Standard Book Number (paper) 0-8014-9593-8
Library of Congress Catalog Card Number 89-627
Printed in the United States of America
Librarians: Library of Congress cataloging information appears on the last page of the book.

The paper in this book is acid-free and meets the guidelines for permanence and durability of the Committee on Production Guidelines for Book Longevity of the Council on Library Resources.

IN MEMORY OF MY FATHER

Roy C. McCall

1906–1989

Contents

"I prefer not to," he respectfully and slowly said, and mildly disappeared.

Preface

While writing this book I was chastened by something I heard at a memorial service for one of my best beloved colleagues. He died a month before he was scheduled to begin his last semester of teaching. A man who had known him for forty years said of him, "He never forgot that the work he was studying was more important than he was."

A practical corollary of that principle is Jacques Barzun's assertion that "the critic's duty is to leave the beholder's soul to its adventure, to its enjoyment":

> It is not the critic's business to disembowel the work by applying to it a doctrine which leaves the reader feeling that the critic's essay is so complete that reading the work itself would be at once superfluous and less comprehensive. The critic, we must never forget, is but a handmaid.[1]

I hope I haven't forgotten, and I have put "Bartleby, The Scrivener" at the end of this book because the story itself is

1. Jacques Barzun, "A Little Matter of Sense," *New York Times Book Review,* June 21, 1987, p. 28.

what we should always be reaching for and coming back to. "Bartleby" is a masterpiece by our most powerful writer, a central text in what we have come to call the American Renaissance, one of the very finest works of short fiction in our literature. By itself, the story warrants—may even require—elaborate analysis. But going through the voluminous criticism and scholarship devoted to "Bartleby," I felt more than once that I had lost the story. I'd lost what got me interested in the first place. So I hope this book provides some illustrative examples of "the critic's duty" and "the critic's business." What I have to say about reading "Bartleby" is about reading Melville, about reading in general, and especially about the way reading is taught in our colleges and universities today. "Bartleby, The Scrivener" is my case in point, and my discussions of it are intended to be paradigmatic.

In each chapter I take up a widely used methodology—source study, psychoanalytic interpretation, Marxist analysis, and so on. My main difficulty with the various critical schools I examine is that they arise, as one of the best writers on the tale suggests, "from the readers' desires to identify and secure Melville within their own rather than his contexts."[2] But what truly counts, as I see it, is Herman Melville's extraordinary achievement in the short story form, his first adventure into that form. When I talk about "the Bartleby Industry," or about myself, I assume the ultimate goal is our shock of recognition when we sit down and read the story itself, on its own terms, bravely and carefully and well.

In presenting the text of the story I have had to make some

2. Milton R. Stern, "Towards 'Bartleby the Scrivener,'" in *The Stoic Strain in American Literature*, ed. Duane J. MacMillan (Toronto: University of Toronto Press, 1979), 19–41, p. 19.

decisions, and I am not altogether confident about some of them. For example, what about the title? And what should we do with the subtitle? When the story first appeared in *Putnam's Monthly Magazine* for November and December, 1853, it was

BARTLEBY, THE SCRIVENER.
A Story of Wall-Street.

When Melville included the story in *The Piazza Tales*, he called it, simply, "Bartleby." Or did he? On January 19, 1856, he wrote to his publisher, Dix and Edwards, that the title of the book would be *Benito Cereno & Other Sketches*, and he proposed a "Table of Contents":

Benito Cereno
Bartleby
Bell-Tower
Encantadas
Lightning-Rod Man[3]

On February 16 Melville wrote his publisher again to say that he had found a new title for the book, *The Piazza Tales;* after the opening piece of that name, "I think, with you, that '*Bartleby*' had best come next." Did he really mean to shorten the title and cut out the subtitle? In both letters, as I read them, he is not deliberately abbreviating the title; he is simply referring to the place the story should occupy in the book. Some critics think "A Story of Wall-Street" is too limiting, that it insists too much on the local setting of a work that has universal implications. Other readers argue the opposite: "Bartleby, The Scrivener" is a story about Wall

3. *The Letters of Herman Melville*, eds. Merrell R. Davis and William H. Gilman (New Haven: Yale University Press, 1960), pp. 179–80.

Street, about economic pressures and class relationships; to remove the subtitle is to remove a cultural dimension from the story which was essential to its imaginative conception.

Melville clearly did mean to change one thing. When the story first appeared in *Putnam's*, the grub-man had a name, "Mr. Cutlets," and he asked Bartleby, "May Mrs. Cutlets and I have the pleasure of your company to dinner, sir, in Mrs. Cutlets' private room?" For *The Piazza Tales*, Melville cut both the name and the dinner invitation. Most modern editors respect these second thoughts. As do I. But should we? A wife, a "Mrs." Anybody, is surely an interesting person to mention in a story in which everybody seems to be a bachelor and the level of sexual energy is about as low as it can get. It does seem a little odd, though, to meet Dame Cutlets here. By the time we have reached this climactic point in the story, there is a woeful hush around everything, a sense of complete withdrawal and ultimate loss. One critic suggests that a note of "inappropriate slap-stick" is introduced by the name "Cutlets" and the reference to a woman's "private room."[4] Then again, that might be just the reason to retain Cutlets and his Mrs. Frequently I ask my students about a detail in Hemingway's "The Killers." Nick Adams comes down the stairs after seeing Ole Andreson turn his face to the wall. Nick says good night to the landlady, Mrs. Hirsch, and she corrects him:

> "I'm not Mrs. Hirsch," the woman said. "She owns the place. I just look after it for her. I'm Mrs. Bell."
>
> "Well, good-night, Mrs. Bell," Nick said.
>
> "Good-night," the woman said.

What a lovely reminder of the mundane, obdurate otherness

4. Egbert Oliver, ed., *The Piazza Tales* (New York: Hendricks House, 1948), p. 230.

of the world. At a time of great dramatic tension, a little meaningless voice whispers in our ear. But "Cutlets" is much louder. Some critics say that is what is good about it, that the name "Cutlets" is symbolically appropriate, altogether in keeping with the names of those other secondary characters "Turkey" and "Nippers" and "Ginger Nut." I think that is just what is wrong with it. Our narrator tells us that the names of his three subordinates are "mutually conferred." Those nicknames belong to the office, and they express its special, feverish intimacy. To carry such names out into the anonymous world, especially to the cold impersonality of the Tombs, seems overclever and falsely insistent.

Finally, the punctuation of the story in the magazine is preferable to the punctuation of the story in the book. The first paragraph has twelve commas in *Putnam's*, thirty in *The Piazza Tales*. On March 24, Melville wrote to his publisher: "There seems to have been a surprising profusion of commas in these proofs. I have struck them out pretty much; but hope that some one who understands punctuation better than I do, will give the final hand to it." Alas, Dix and Edwards ignored both Melville's own excisions and his request for help.[5]

My gratitude to those who have faithfully given me encouragement and criticism, especially M. H. Abrams, Melissa Bank, Jonathan Bishop, Allan Emery, Joel Porte, Edgar Rosenberg, Mark Seltzer, Bert O. States, and Milton R. Stern.

DAN MCCALL

Ithaca, New York

5. *Letters*, p. 180. As to the other very minor changes, I usually prefer the 1853 version, e.g., the grub-man's reference to "spacious grounds" rather than "nice grounds." It seems to me a toss-up in the last paragraph between the 1853 "I cannot adequately express" and the 1856 "hardly can I express."

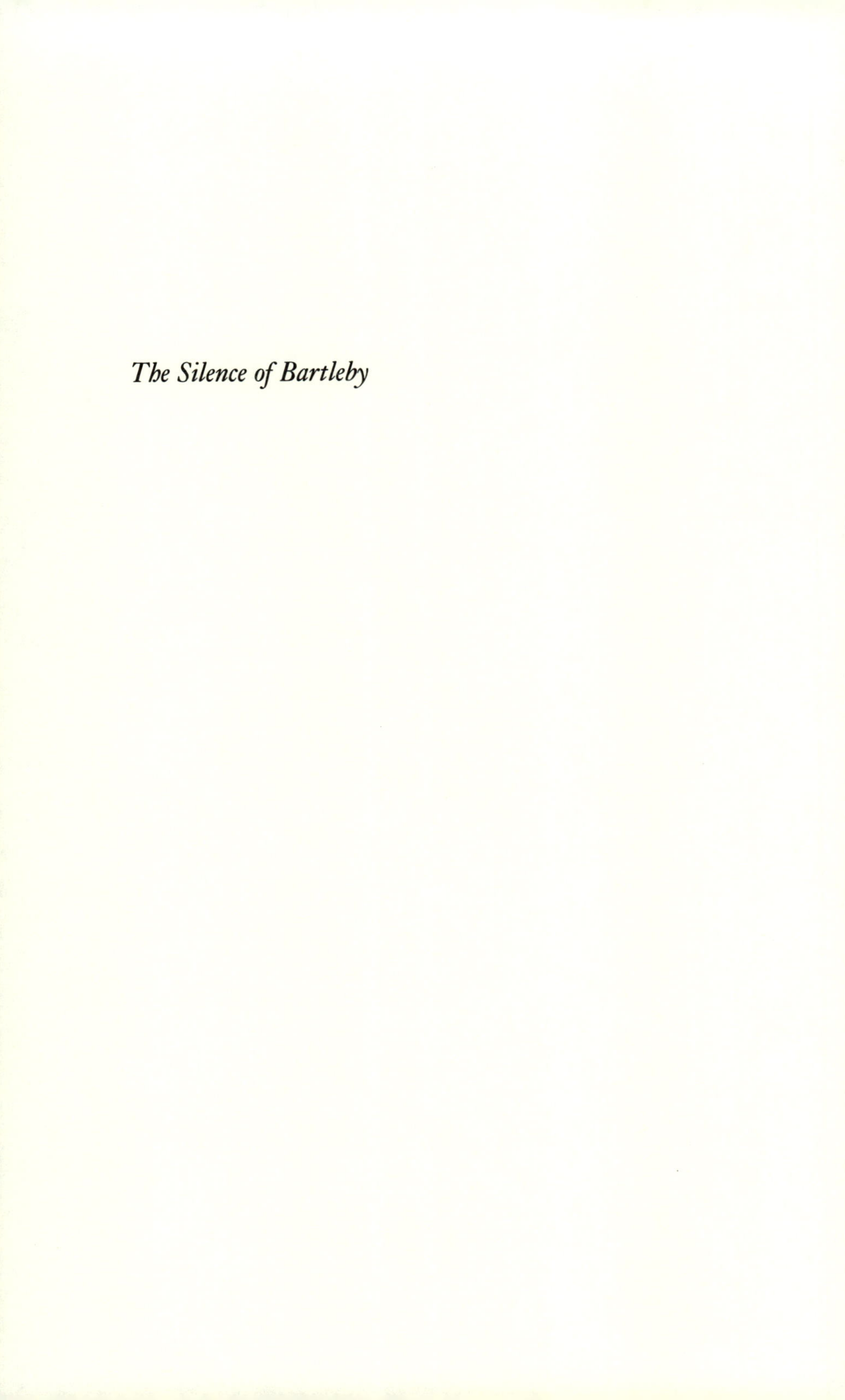

The Silence of Bartleby

CHAPTER I

Swimming through Libraries

I have swam through libraries and sailed through oceans; I have had to do with whales with these visible hands; I am in earnest; and I will try.

Moby-Dick

I should like to begin by examining three sources for "Bartleby, The Scrivener"—an article in a newspaper, some verses in the Bible, and an essay by Emerson. Simply on the basis of strong similarities in language, one can see that Melville used all three of them. But exactly how he came to use them, what they may tell us, separately and together, about the way his mind worked, and how they function artistically in "Bartleby" are difficult questions to answer.

The first item is "The Lawyer's Story; Or, the Wrongs of the Orphans. By a Member of the Bar." Discovered by Johannes Dietrich Bergmann, it is a full-page article in both the *New York Times* and the *New York Tribune*, February 18, 1853, some months before Melville began writing "Bartleby."[1] I think anyone who has read "Bartleby" carefully will tremble a little when reading the first sentence of the newspaper story:

1. Johannes Dietrich Bergmann, "Bartleby and *The Lawyer's Story*," *American Literature*, 47 (1975), 432–36.

The Silence of Bartleby

> In the summer of 1843, having an extraordinary quantity of deeds to copy, I engaged, temporarily, an extra copying clerk, who interested me considerably, in consequence of his modest, quiet, gentlemanly demeanor, and in his intense application to his duties.

This clerk was "singularly sedate in aspect"; he copied with "incessant industry," and to his employer's questions he answered, "I would prefer." We are told that "the young man's countenance was shaded with constitutional or habitual melancholy," and he "declined telling who he was, or whence he came, or whether he had any relatives in the world." When he said, "Hope for the future is dead within me," the lawyer replied, "I urge you to view the matter differently. You are a young man; brilliant prospects may be before you; happiness may yet await you." That is Melville's Lawyer, encouraging Bartleby to try new things. Throughout the article, this anonymous lawyer talks very much like Melville's: "I could not get this out of my head the whole day. It haunted me so much as to perplex me in my business; and yet, cogitate as I might I could find no reason for it." Melville's Lawyer resolves to tell Bartleby that "if in any other way I could assist him, I would be happy to do so," and "Moreover, if, after reaching home, he found himself at any time in want of aid, a letter from him would be sure of a reply." The lawyer in the newspaper story offers to write his clerk a letter of "recommendation, assuring him that I would do all in my power to afford him assistance." Here surely, is our melancholy extra copyist, here are some key lines, and here is the Lawyer-narrator himself.

There are some significant differences between the newspaper story and what Melville made out of it. In the newspaper the lawyer tells us that perhaps "melancholy" was not "constitutional" with this young copyist because "when anything deeply interested him, this expression disappeared, and left in its place an earnest and winning smile." That is certainly not Bartleby. And the original is about a brother and sister, Adolphus and Georgianna Fitzherbert; Melville did not want the sister. In the newspaper the lawyer has a smiling wife; very well, then, get rid of the wife. And one has to wonder if Bartleby's "I would prefer not to" can really be said to find its origin here. In the newspaper, "I would prefer" (not "I would prefer not to") occurs just once, buried deep in a lengthy dialogue in which the young man rambles on about all sorts of things and merely says, "I would prefer being near my sister." The line has no prominence, no emphasis at all.

But there are so many things in the newspaper that do shed light on key passages in Melville's story. For example, a line that has occasioned strong disagreement among critics is the Lawyer's claim in the opening paragraph of "Bartleby" that he has known many law-copyists and "if I pleased, could relate divers histories, at which good-natured gentlemen might smile, and sentimental souls might weep." The source for the line seems to be in the newspaper story in two places, one near the beginning and one at the very end. The concluding promise in the newspaper story is that "from the incidents I learnt, I shall weave the whole affair into a narrative" and, earlier, "I related the story to my wife. It was one well calculated to enlist the sympathy of women." Melville's Lawyer thinks that "Bartleby was billeted upon me for some mysterious purpose of an all-wise Providence, which it was not for a mere mortal like me to fathom." In the newspaper, the lawyer exclaims to the copyist's sister that "Providence" must have "ordered it for some wise purpose we cannot divine." Surely this is a source for the line in "Bartleby": Providence/Providence, purpose/purpose, fathom/divine.

Consider, as a second example, something altogether different but just as convincing. In *The Wake of the Gods*, Bruce Franklin proposes that "Bartleby" illustrates point by point Christ's injunction in Matthew 25:34–40:[2]

> Then shall the King say unto them on his right hand, Come, ye blessed of my Father, inherit the kingdom prepared for you from the foundation of the world:
>
> For I was an hungred, and ye gave me meat; I was thirsty, and ye gave me drink: I was a stranger, and ye took me in:
>
> Naked, and ye clothed me: I was sick, and ye visited me; I was in prison, and ye came unto me.
>
> Then shall the righteous answer him, saying, Lord, when saw we thee an hungred, and fed *thee?* or thirsty, and gave *thee* drink?
>
> When saw we thee a stranger, and took *thee* in? or naked, and clothed *thee?*
>
> Or when saw we thee sick, or in prison, and came unto thee?
>
> And the King shall answer and say unto them, Verily I say unto you, Inasmuch as ye have done *it* unto one of the least of these my brethren, ye have done *it* unto me.

Now this does not quite work. The Lawyer does not clothe Bartleby (though he does try to give Turkey an old overcoat); the Lawyer does not give Bartleby meat or drink (though he worries a lot about Bartleby's diet). But Bartleby is a stranger, and the Lawyer takes him in; the Lawyer knows Bartleby is sick and tries to help him; Bartleby is taken to prison, and the Lawyer comes unto him. Christ insists we do these things to "the least of these"—and Bartleby is "this forlornest of mankind." All the words are different, but they powerfully mean the same thing. Franklin notes a recurrent series of puns in Melville's story ("elec-

2. Bruce Franklin, *The Wake of the Gods* (Stanford, Calif.: Stanford University Press, 1963), pp. 126–36.

tion," "advent," "passion"); the narrator does think of "the divine injunction: 'A new commandment give I unto you, that ye love one another.' " In the Gospel according to Mark, Christ is sent to prison and "numbered with the transgressors"; Bartleby is incarcerated amid "murderers and thieves." When the going gets tough for the Lawyer, and his friends chastise him, he denies Bartleby—denies him three times:

> One: "but, really, the man you allude to is nothing to me—"
>
> Two: "I certainly cannot inform you. I know nothing about him."
>
> Three: "In vain I persisted that Bartleby was nothing to me—"

In Mark 14:71, Peter says, "I know not this man of whom ye speak." That is awfully close to "the man you allude to is nothing to me." And *three times*—not two, not four.

Franklin cautiously and correctly adds that "this is a tragic story no matter who the being is," and if we "read *Bartleby* well, we must first realize that we can never know who or what Bartleby is, but that we are continually asked to guess who or what he might be." I reread the evidence Franklin had put before me and found myself worrying that the language of denial seemed more convincing in Matthew than in Mark; then, with a start, I realized I was doing it sideways, weighing Matthew against Mark, instead of seeing both in "Bartleby." I was picking at each of Franklin's details—should we really see a pun in the "Master's" office? Should we see Jesus in the call for "additional help," or the Lawyer's inability to find "anything ordinarily human about him" or the conclusion that Bartleby has "nothing else earthly to do"? But Franklin's summary of his thesis, that the whole story comes from Matthew 25, is elegantly persuasive: "The narrator fulfills the letter of Christ's injunction point by point: he offers money to the stranger so that he may eat and drink; he takes him in, finally offering him not only his office but also his home; when he sees that he is sick he attempts to minister to him; he, alone of all mankind, visits and befriends the stranger in prison." One can see the rich general conception, and one can hear the clear verbal echoes.

Let me turn to a third example before I consider the general problem. "The Mast-Head" chapter in *Moby-Dick* concludes with a portrait of an "absent minded youth" up in the crow's nest of the ship; he suddenly "loses his identity" by blending the cadences of the waves with his own thoughts, and he "takes the mystic ocean at his feet for the visible image of that deep, blue, bottomless soul, pervading mankind and nature." With "one half-throttled shriek" he drops "through that transparent air into the summer sea, no more to rise for ever." Whenever I read this remarkable passage I think of Emerson's *Nature*. I am almost positive Melville was thinking about it.[3] And I am almost positive he was thinking of another Emerson essay when he was writing "Bartleby." In "The Transcendentalist" Emerson says:

> It is a sign of our times, conspicuous to the coarsest observer, that many intelligent and religious persons withdraw themselves from the common labors and competitions of the market and the caucus, and betake themselves to a certain solitary and critical way of living, from which no solid fruit has yet appeared to justify their separation. They hold themselves aloof. . . . They are lonely; the spirit of their writing and conversation is lonely; they repel influences; they shun general society; they incline to shut themselves in

3. He heard Emerson lecture in the winter of 1848–49, and in 1850 he read some of Emerson's essays when he was revising *Moby-Dick*.

their chamber in the house . . . to find their tasks and amusements in solitude. Society, to be sure, does not like this very well; it saith, Whoso goes to walk alone, accuses the whole world; he declares all to be unfit to be his companions.

Is this somewhere on Melville's mind when he conceives his story?[4] Emerson speaks of a young man, lonely and withdrawn, with whom a paternal figure talks at great length, pleadingly, but cannot reach. That is the essential idea of "Bartleby." The wiser, older man's voice rises with resentment when he can produce no response in the young man—"it is very uncivil, nay, insulting"—and we can feel Emerson's exasperation, so like the Lawyer's in "Bartleby." Emerson does what the Lawyer does: the character of the young man "inspires a new interest in our own," and he feels it with such "vivacity of apprehension . . . that I am instantly forced home to inquire if I am not deformity itself." Bartleby makes the Lawyer question his own life, and feel very troubled, even ashamed, about it. Solitary young men, aloof and fastidious, are too much trouble "because of the extravagant demand they make on human nature."

Sophia Hawthorne wrote to her sister, Elizabeth Peabody, that on one visit Melville "shut himself into the boudoir and read Mr. Emerson's essays" all one morning.[5] It may not have been that day, in the early fall of 1850, but surely one day before he composed "Bartleby" Melville read "The Transcendentalist" with considerable care. The very last

4. See Christopher W. Sten, "Bartleby the Transcendentalist: Melville's Dead Letter to Emerson," *Modern Language Quarterly*, 35 (March, 1974), 30–44. Sten and I see many of the same things, but we don't interpret them in the same way, and we draw different conclusions. I use "The Transcendentalist" in *Selections from Ralph Waldo Emerson*, ed. Stephen E. Whicher (Boston: Houghton Mifflin, 1960), 192–206.

5. Quoted in Sten, "Bartleby the Transcendentalist," p. 31.

line of his story could have been inspired by Emerson's phrase, "his name should be the prayer I should utter to the Universe." Emerson's young idealists "cannot gossip with you, and they do not wish, as they are sincere and religious, to gratify any mere curiosity which you may entertain. Like fairies, they do not wish to be spoken of. Love me, they say, but do not ask who is my cousin and my uncle." Similarly, Bartleby "declined telling who he was, or whence he came, or whether he had any relatives in the world." When the Lawyer asks him "what is the reason?" for his behavior, Bartleby replies, "Do you not see the reason for yourself?" That answer seems to come from "The Transcendentalist," in which the young man responds to the sage's question by saying that "you do not need to hear my thought, because you can read it in my face" and "if you cannot divine it, you would not understand what I say." How like Bartleby's blandly defiant answers are the bleak sentences of the young man: "I will not molest myself for you. I do not wish to be profaned." We can hear Bartleby the *scrivener* in Emerson's young man: "I do not wish to perform it. I do not wish to do one thing but once. I do not love routine."

Not only individual lines—whole dialogues! The Lawyer's interrogations of Bartleby begin in Emerson's imagined colloquies about how "we are miserable with inaction. We perish of rest and rust: but we do not like your work":

> "Then," says the world, "show me your own."
> "We have none."
> "What will you do, then?" cries the world.
> "We will wait."
> "How long?"
> "Until the Universe beckons and calls us to work."
> "But whilst you wait, you grow old and useless."
> "Be it so: I can sit in a corner and *perish* (as you call it), but I will not move . . . your virtuous projects, so called, do not cheer me."

The structure and substance of what is going on here is remarkably similar to the conversations between the Lawyer and Bartleby. The man asking questions of the young idealist is "the man of the world," who eventually learns that his society "must behold with what charity it can" such young men as these. Emerson speaks of his forlorn idealist as a "storm-tossed vessel at sea," and the Lawyer speaks of Bartleby as "a bit of wreck in the mid Atlantic." Clearly, Emerson's "The Transcendentalist," like "The Lawyer's Story" in the newspaper and the Book of Matthew in the Bible, is a source for "Bartleby." There are unmistakable traces of all three in Melville's general conception and in his specific scenes; there are abundant echoes of all three in his prose.

But how far can we go with all this? And to what purpose? I find it difficult to read "Bartleby" with any one of these "sources" in mind—I doubt that I *can* read "Bartleby" with all three of them jostling my attention. After decades of extremely productive work, "the Bartleby Industry" has put us in a rather peculiar position: the more we see of what went into the story, the less we understand the story itself. Each new discovery seems only to complicate and baffle our ability to read "Bartleby" coherently.

When Emerson withdrew from his divinity studies at Harvard, he said, "My eyes refused to read." That marvelous verb, "refused," puts in the active mode what the young scholar experiences passively: lethargy, eyestrain, general ill health, and nagging doubt about his fitness for an awesome vocation. "My eyes refused to read" converts all that trouble into focused spiritual rebellion: the texts Emerson was reading were intolerable to him, for they said things he could not believe. When I read some of the more extravagant critical interpretations of "Bartleby, The Scrivener" I find myself stuck in a version of what Emerson said of his own terrible fix. For example, in *Atlantic Double-Cross: Amer-*

ican Literature and British Influence in the Age of Emerson, Robert Weisbuch proposes in an essay on "Bartleby" that "Melville's lawyer, that 'eminently *safe* man,' is Charles Dickens, an eminently safe writer who never delves beneath the social construct to question the abyss of existence."[6] I instinctively distrust this kind of identification (the Lawyer *is* Dickens?), and I distrust, too, that characterization of Dickens himself. Brian Foley, a student of Weisbuch, suggests Melville was jealous because Dickens was more famous than he. In Foley's view, Melville's "goal is not so much parody as one-upmanship," his "purpose is to show not just an American can write a Dickensian story as well as Dickens can, but that he can write one better. . . . Melville was motivated by professional jealousy," for Dickens's fame in America "was surely a bitter pill for Melville to swallow."[7] Confronting such an argument I find my eyes refusing to read. Foley says he has found "additional proof that the narrator is not sincere."[8] Can one really "prove" anything about a fictional character's sincerity? Scholarly interpretations and critical opinions are often presented in this false armor of irrefutable "evidence." When critics persuade themselves that they are dealing with *facts*, they forget the distinction E. B. White makes in *The Elements of Style:*

> *Fact.* Use this word only of matter capable of direct verification, not of matters of judgment. That a particular event happened on a given date, that lead melts at a certain temperature are facts. But

6. Robert Weisbuch, "Melville's 'Bartleby' and the Dead Letter of Charles Dickens," in *Atlantic Double-Cross: American Literature and British Influence in the Age of Emerson* (Chicago: University of Chicago Press, 1986), p. 43.

7. Brian Foley, "Dickens Revised: 'Bartleby' and *Bleak House*," *Essays in Literature*, 12 (Fall, 1985), 247.

8. Ibid., p. 249, n. 10.

such conclusions as that Napoleon was the greatest of modern generals or that the climate of California is delightful, however defensible they may be, are not properly called facts.[9]

Michael H. Friedman tells us that in Dickens a "bagman's uncle meditates upon the 'dead' mail coaches much as the narrator of Bartleby meditates upon the dead letters," but that the "displacement" of the mail coach by the letters contained in them "has helped to disguise Melville's literary debt to Dickens."[10] First, those quotation marks around "dead" are misleading—"dead" is Friedman's word, not Dickens's. But, more important, one wonders what would be the purpose of such "disguise." If Friedman and Foley are both correct, then we have a curious situation in which Melville seems to be simultaneously concealing and displaying his material. If one doubts he would perform either maneuver, it is a little difficult to see him doing both.

To be sure, he was reading Dickens—everybody in America was. *Harper's New Monthly Magazine*, to which Melville subscribed, serialized *Bleak House* from April 1852 to October 1853, and Melville wrote "Bartleby" in the summer of 1853. A review of "Bartleby" said it was "equal to anything" of Dickens, and "closely resembles" Dickens "both as to the character of the sketch and the peculiarity of the style."[11] And we can see shadows of *Bleak House* all over Melville's Wall Street office.

In his pamphlet, *"Bartleby the Scrivener" and "Bleak House": Melville's Debt to Dickens*, David Jaffe has shown how

9. William Strunk, Jr., and E. B. White, *The Elements of Style* (New York: Macmillan, 1979), p. 46.

10. Michael H. Friedman, "*Pickwick Papers* as a Source for the Epilogue to Melville's 'Bartleby, the Scrivener,'" *Studies in Short Fiction*, 21 (Spring, 1984), 147–51, p. 150.

11. Review of *The Piazza Tales* in the *Daily Evening Traveler*, June 3, 1856.

"Nemo," the pathetic copyist in *Bleak House*, works night and day at "folios" and leaves "no more track behind him than anyone can trace" and who, when found dead, at first seems to be asleep. Melville's Turkey closely resembles Mr. Boythorn (these two elderly Englishmen sport radiant countenances and are always putting up their fists). Melville's second scrivener, Nippers, like Dickens's second scrivener, Guppy, has trouble adjusting himself to his desk. And Dickens's young Smallweed, whose grandfather is "made a clerk in a sharp scrivener's office at twelve years old," is Ginger Nut, the same age, "some twelve years old," whose father sent him to the office as a clerk.[12] Any one of these might seem insubstantial, but as with Franklin's survey of Melville's use of biblical puns, their accumulated weight is what counts. Jaffe points out that both in Melville and in Dickens we have "blank walls," "blinded" walls, "dead walls," and a character who frequently stands with "his head against a wall." What is particularly striking to me is that Dickens's high house is like an "oblong cistern to hold the fog"; Wall Street does not have any London fogs, but Melville retains the "cistern" between the buildings: that is, even lacking fog to catch, a fantasy cistern persists.

There is Dickens, to be sure, in abundance. But why does that mean Melville's lawyer "is" Dickens? Weisbuch goes on to say that Dickens "is only the Lawyer's ultimate identification, and in the course of Melville's story he bears two other identities as well." On the way to his ultimate identification, the Lawyer's "very lack of a personal name suggests the degree to which his selfhood has been usurped by his occupation."[13] I wonder. Does Melville deliberately leave out personal names to "suggest" usurpation of "selfhood"? But

12. David Jaffe, *"Bartleby the Scrivener" and "Bleak House"* (Hamden Court: Archon, 1979). See especially p. 10.

13. Weisbuch, *Atlantic Double-Cross*, p. 43.

we have those "two other identities" waiting for us, and "Dickensian prose is momentarily discarded" when Melville has quite another writer in mind:

> Again I sat ruminating what I should do. Mortified as I was at his behavior, and resolved as I had been to dismiss him when I entered my office, nevertheless I strangely felt something superstitious knocking at my heart, and forbidding me to carry out my purpose, and denouncing me for a villain if I dared to breathe one bitter word against this forlornest of mankind.

Weisbuch says, "These are the cadences, this the lexicon of Edgar Allan Poe." Perhaps it is the "something superstitious" Weisbuch hears as Poe, but I do not, and as for the "lexicon," Poe surely would not call Bartleby "this forlornest of mankind." Weisbuch's final identification is with a man who "like Bartleby in Melville's words 'had been suddenly removed by a change in the administration.' The man, of course, is Hawthorne. If the Lawyer is someways Dickens at his worst, Bartleby is a failed Hawthorne."[14] So we have a trio: Dickens, Poe, and Hawthorne, all slaving away on Wall Street.

Like a jack-in-the-box, the figure of Poe pops up repeatedly in the critical commentary: "Bartleby" is a "Gothic thriller"; Bartleby himself is Roderick Usher, with "boundless, terrifying potential" and the Lawyer's office is "as clearly destructive to human life as any Gothic mansion."[15] A pair of critics goes so far as to read Bartleby's "I prefer not to" as a deliberate jibe at Poe: "Bartleby has indeed 'quoth nevermore.'"[16] After all, Melville's Lawyer has a bust of

14. Ibid., p. 53.

15. Steven T. Ryan, "The Gothic Formula of 'Bartleby,'" *Arizona Quarterly*, 34 (Winter, 1978), 311–16, pp. 313–14.

16. James L. Colwell and Gary Spitzer, "'Bartleby' and 'The Raven': Parallels of the Irrational," *Georgia Review*, 23 (Spring, 1969), 37–43, p. 40.

Cicero in his office, and Poe's raven perches on a bust of Athena. These statuesque associations are reinforced by another critic, who notes that Melville made fun of Poe in *The Confidence Man*'s queer little "shatter-brain" with "raven [!] curls," the "crazy" and "cracked" little fellow with his "frock coat buttoned up to the chin" just the way Poe famously buttoned up his coat.[17] We have no evidence that Melville and Poe ever actually met but they did both live in New York in the late 1840s, and Evert Duyckinck served as adviser to both. Perhaps Duyckinck himself was the anonymous critic who called "Bartleby" a "Poeish tale" in the *Literary World* of December 3, 1853.

Another critic takes that baton and runs with it: "The lawyer *is* Duyckinck, for Duyckinck rejected Melville as the lawyer rejected Bartleby." After all, Melville canceled his subscription to the *Literary World* in an abrupt note to Duyckinck. We can see that "'the master's office' is, of course, the editorship of a literary journal."[18] Looking closely, you can see that even the minor characters are in on it—Turkey is Cornelius Matthews and now it is Nippers who is Edgar Allan Poe.

"Bartleby" is a fantasia of literary gossip. Critics "prove" that Bartleby is Melville himself, and Edgar Allan Poe, and Nathaniel Hawthorne. Later, in my third chapter, I shall consider an entire subsection of the Bartleby Industry, impressive in its size and ingenuity, which "proves" that Bartleby is Henry David Thoreau. Bartleby is also "proved" to be two personal friends of Melville, and it is suggested that he is based on two well-known lunatics who had wandered

17. Harrison Hayford, "Poe in 'The Confidence Man,'" *Nineteenth-Century Fiction*, 14 (1959), 207–18, p. 207.

18. Daniel A. Wells, "'Bartleby the Scrivener,' Poe, and the Duyckinck Circle," *Emerson Society Quarterly*, 21 (1975), 35–39, p. 36.

the New York City streets. He is even a "slave" (one commentator challenges us to prove Bartleby isn't black). Bartleby is a phantom who doesn't exist at all except as the narrator's death wish. And Jesus Christ, of course. Similarly, the quiet, self-effacing Lawyer-narrator is "proved" to be not only Charles Dickens but also Ralph Waldo Emerson, Washington Irving, Poe again, Hawthorne again, Melville himself again, Melville's father-in-law Lemuel Shaw, Duyckinck, and even Pontius Pilate. Nobody in Melville's tale is safe as himself or "means" who he literally is. Bartleby is "a nightmare creature who drives God into self-knowledge," God being the Old Testament Jehovah who through the experience of Bartleby becomes "the New Testament God of love."[19] Enlisted in this heavenly free-for-all, poor Turkey is "the militant archangel Michael," his ruler his sword, and Nippers is Lucifer, and little Ginger Nut is Milton's Raphael who brings "the official cake (or 'wafer') and apple (forbidden fruit)."

One critic has suggested that the characters represent, in Melville's anatomy of melancholy, the four humours: Turkey is sanguine, Nippers choleric, the Lawyer phlegmatic, and Bartleby melancholic.[20] Bartleby is not a man but a "subliminal death drive" who has "merely emerged from the lawyer's mind."[21] Richard Harter Fogle sees Nippers as "Sir Gawaine, whose strength grew steadily till midday and then

19. John Gardner, "Bartleby: Art and Social Commitment," *Philological Quarterly*, 43 (January, 1964), 87–98, pp. 95–96.

20. Nathalia Wright, "Melville and 'Old Burton,' with 'Bartleby' as an Anatomy of Melancholy," *Tennessee Studies in English*, 15 (1970), 1–13. I do not mean to scorn the suggestion, for Melville liked to play these little games, and he was especially good at this one. "Old Burton" was a favorite author; Melville treasured his father's copy of the *Anatomy of Melancholy*.

21. Mordecai Marcus, "Melville's Bartleby as Psychological Double," *College English*, 23 (1962), 365–68, p. 366.

declined"—and because Turkey is English and Nippers American, they are "national types according to the mythology of the nineteenth-century," John Bull and Yankee.[22] Another critic goes so far as to say that because the Englishman, Turkey, is in his ascendancy before noon and the American, Nippers, is in his during the afternoon, "Melville here is predicting the decline of England and the subsequent rise of America."[23] But how can that be? When we check back with the story, we find that Melville says Nippers is Turkey's "compatriot." I suppose that could mean they are "compatriots" as fellow scriveners, not countrymen, but still, we might hesitate to predict the rise and fall of empires.

Consider the name "Bartleby" itself. In the critical commentary we can see it "proved" to be:

"Bartlemy," from Lamb's essay on "St. Bartholomew."

"Barney," Melville's pet name for his son Malcolm.

"Bounderby," from *Hard Times*. (There is a little problem here, since "Bartleby, The Scrivener" was published in 1853, and *Hard Times* was written in 1854).

"Bartle-*B*," from Priestly's Son "A" and Son "B."

"*B*-ing" itself, since Melville wrote *B-enito Cereno* and *B-illy B-udd*, as well as *B-artle-By*, and was always questioning our essential *B*-ing.

All of the above? None of the above?

It is always possible that we have on our hands a bewildering array of in-jokes, private references never intended to be understood by the common reader. Harrison Hayford

22. Richard Harter Fogle, *Melville's Shorter Tales* (Norman: University of Oklahoma Press, 1960), 16–18.

23. Foley, "Dickens Revised," p. 247.

speaks of Melville's "habitual practice, perhaps a necessity of his creative method, of writing from experience, observation and reading, rather than from pure invention. The greater part of his characters seem to have originals, not all of whom he intended or wished to be recognized."[24] And Leon Howard reminds us that in *Mardi*'s elaborate flower symbolism "Melville was communicating more to his bride than he ever expected the public to understand."[25] Frequently Melville was less than candid about the way he used other men's books. Writing *White Jacket*, he elaborately "stole" from James Mercier's *Life in a Man of War;* writing *Omoo*, he copied extensively from Ellis's *Polynesian Researches.* And he constantly covers his tracks: in *Typee* he claims he "never happened to meet with" Porter's *Journal of a Cruise Made to the Pacific Ocean in the U.S. Frigate Essex.* But, of course, he did happen to meet with it. He is full of little borrowings and big ones.

If we set out to "prove" that any one of these borrowings has primacy over the others, on what basis do we do so? Do we decide each case on its merits, welcoming some of the sources and discarding others? Is there some kind of general principle at work? I have mentioned my dismay at trying to keep in my head just the three items I began with. The difficulty is not only the wide range of material but also the kinds of material—a reader of "Bartleby" does not think of "The Lawyer's Story" in the New York newspaper the way he might think of the Book of Matthew. Whether he may think of Emerson is another question. And how do we juggle all of these other balls that the Bartleby Industry keeps throwing to us? There seems to be no end to them!

24. Hayford, "Poe in 'The Confidence Man,'" p. 215.

25. Leon Howard, *Herman Melville: A Biography* (Berkeley: University of California Press, 1951), p. 115.

For example, several critics argue that "Bartleby" reflects Melville's immersion in the work of Washington Irving. Late in his life Melville dedicated a little piece, "Rip Van Winkle's Lilac," to the "happy shade" of Irving. One reader asserts that the wise old chronicler of Knickerbocker Days "set standards of composition which Melville preferred rather to be annihilated than to copy," but Irving was nevertheless on Melville's mind: "the easiest way of life is the best" is Melville's sly allusion to Irving at Sunnyside in "the cool tranquillity of a snug retreat."[26] Melville expected his readers to get it when he wrote that his Lawyer (like Washington Irving) had been employed and trusted by John Jacob Astor. Already, in *Mardi*, he had parodied the codicils of Astor's will. In the early stages of their friendship Duyckinck found Melville to be a man who "models his writing a great deal on that of Washington Irving."[27] When *Typee* was about to appear in London, Irving was there on a visit; he read the proof sheets and expressed confidence in the book's success. Melville acquired two volumes of Irving in June, 1853, right before he began writing "Bartleby."

In the most famous of his literary essays, "Hawthorne and His Mosses," Melville referred to Washington Irving as "that graceful writer, who perhaps of all Americans has received the most plaudits from his own country"; he is "that very popular and amiable writer" who owes his fame to the self-acknowledged imitation of a foreign model—Goldsmith—"and to the studied avoidance of all topics but smooth ones." There is the Lawyer, insisting on his "eminently *safe*" life. R. Bruce Bickley, Jr., shows us that "Irving's presence is

26. Martin Pops, quoted in *Bartleby the Inscrutable: A Collection of Commentary on Herman Melville's Tale "Bartleby the Scrivener,"* ed. M. Thomas Inge (Hamden, Conn.: Archon Books, 1979). See Lewis Leary's introductory essay, p. 16.

27. Quoted in Howard, *Herman Melville*, p. 107.

chiefly felt in the narrative technique" of "Bartleby"; the Lawyer is a kind of Jeffrey Crayon of *The Sketchbook:* "The basic similarities between Irving's and Melville's tales are in matters of narrative perspective. Essentially, the 'bachelor' is the controlling consciousness in Irving."[28] He is a man who talks about his estrangement from "life," in just the same way the Lawyer does on the opening pages of "Bartleby."

This is not a little private joke; a literate person in America in the early 1850s knew about the author of "The Legend of Sleepy Hollow"; a literate person would hear *Astoria* in the Lawyer's proud boast that he was employed in his "profession by the late John Jacob Astor; a name which, I admit, I love to repeat." We are on the right track here: "I will freely add, that I was not insensible to the late John Jacob Astor's good opinion." Washington Irving surely was not insensible; he was on contract, and took a $10,000 bonus from Astor for *Astoria.* Moreover, as Bickley points out, in Irving's *Tales of a Traveller* a young Italian is "physically similar to Bartleby in his pallor, emaciation, and haggardness of brow," a man who keeps to himself; "to the narrator the young man appears 'tormented by some fancy or apprehension' and is afflicted with 'a devouring melancholy.' "[29] Irving's "The Little Man in Black" in *Salmagundi* is very Bartlebyish, too, even to the odd detail of the sequel. It is the story of a silent little guy who drives a whole town crazy by his mysterious inaccessibility, just the way Bartleby drives the Wall Street office crazy. We can see traces of this in the "extremely little man" whom the sailors on the *Highlander* try to figure out in *Redburn.*[30] Melville is obviously leafing back and forth in his

28. R. Bruce Bickley, Jr., "'Bartleby' as Paradigm," *The Method of Melville's Shorter Tales* (Durham, N.C.: Duke University Press, 1979), pp. 27–29.

29. Ibid., p. 31.

30. John Seelye, "The Contemporary Bartleby," *American Transcendental Quarterly,* 7 (Summer, 1970), 12–18.

newly acquired volume of Irving; in "The Adventure of The Mysterious Stranger" (Mark Twain too?) the Italian "seemed content to carry his load of misery in silence, and only sought to carry it by my side. There was a mute beseeching manner about him, as if he craved companionship as a charitable boon." This "mysterious stranger" begins to have an effect upon the narrator that is similar to the effect Bartleby has on the Lawyer. Irving's narrator says: "I felt this melancholy to be infectious. It stole over my spirits; interfered with all my gay pursuits, and gradually saddened my life; yet I could not prevail upon myself to shake off a being who seemed to lean upon me for support." We cannot make too much of this, for Melville is clearly and deeply involved with Washington Irving.

But when we consult the original Irving texts, we find our young Italian suffering from a bad case of romantic agony: "he panted rather than breathed; his eyes were bloodshot." He is not at all like Bartleby; he is "feverish" and "livid" and terribly talkative, exploding into fits of gush. If anything, he is the opposite of Bartleby: "his bounty was lavish and openhanded, his charity melting and spontaneous." Our young Italian babbles on about "monastic grievances and disgusts" and a wildly misspent youth. And "The Little Man in Black" is not who the critics said he was. There is no narrator; the little man himself is a pious Christian. Bartleby never breathes a word about where he comes from; Irving's "Little Man in Black" is all ancestor worship, proclaiming that "in me you behold the last descendant of the renowned Linkum Fiedelius." He is not recalcitrant or obdurate or implacable. Irving's sketch is not a source for Bartleby in the sense that "The Lawyer's Story" or the Book of Matthew or "The Transcendentalist" is. The problem is not that certain little pieces do not fit a general design; rather, we find ourselves straining to locate the little pieces.

Perhaps some critics, persuaded of the general claim that Melville is "bookish," are too eager to claim fame for their "discoveries." If you go far enough along those lines, you begin to hypnotize yourself with details until you see things that are not even there. That seems to be the case in a two-page article, "Don Quixote and Melville's 'Bartleby, The Scrivener.'"[31] We learn that Sancho Panza meets a bandit who "serenely insists that even if he is thrown in jail all mankind will not be able to make him sleep, *if he prefers not to.*" What? Say it again? Well, he does say it again, the line is there *twice* (italics in the original): "*If I prefer not to sleep and stay wide awake all night without slamming an eyelid down, will your grace suffice with all your power to make me sleep, if I prefer not to?*" That slamming eyelid looks a little suspicious, and our critic acknowledges that Melville did not acquire the book until 1855. But the famous Jarvis translation of *Don Quixote* was published in 1853. *Two* "I prefer not to"s are compelling. Melville would not expect his readers to get it, of course, but that is surely where he got it.

Or did he? When I finally located the passage in the old Jarvis translation, I found that it read, "If I choose not to sleep, can your worship, with all your power, force me to sleep?" "Choose" once? Not "I prefer not to" twice? I went back to my modern critic, and rechecked his claim that "here, then, in embryonic form is a provocative prefiguration of Melville's stoic Bartleby, who constantly reiterated his stance with the words 'I would prefer not to.'" But, buried down in a footnote, in parentheses, is "I translate." If "*I* translate," what is all the fuss about Jarvis? I knew that eyelid should not have slammed down. It is not Jarvis. It is not really Cervantes. And it is certainly not Melville.

I stumbled across an innocent example of self-hypnotism

31. Fred Abrams, "Don Quixote and Melville's 'Bartleby, The Scrivener,'" *Studies in Short Fiction*, 18 (Summer, 1981), 323–24.

when I was reading the *Letters* to see if Melville wrote to anyone about reading Dickens. By heart I had his letter to Duyckinck about reading Shakespeare: "I am mad to think how minute a cause has prevented me hitherto from reading Shakespeare. But until now any copy that was come-atable to me happened to be in a vile small print unendurable to my eyes which are tender as young sperms." Always I use that letter when I teach *Moby-Dick*—that fantastic last word "sperms"; I use it when I discuss "A Squeeze of the Hand" and "The Cassock." I read the letter again and was moving on to check out Dickens when I suddenly stopped and went back. Melville's letter, in the great edition of Davis and Gilman, says: "any copy that was come-atable to me happened to be in a vile small print unendurable to my eyes which are tender as young sparrows."[32] Sparrows? I know not sparrows. Have I been misteaching *Moby-Dick* for twenty years? Charles Olson quotes the letter so tellingly in *Call Me Ishmael*. Did Olson simply misread it? But how could anybody misread *sperms* for *sparrows?* Or maybe Davis and Gilman have it wrong? Melville's eyes did not refuse to read, his eyes read voraciously, poor man, his eyes tender as young . . .? Is this like Matthiessen's famous "coiled fish"/ "soiled fish" blooper, where Melville's immersion in the metaphysical poets was actually just a printer's error?

But, again, however interesting these little matters are, they do not present what seems to me the challenging problem of how Melville's earnest study and casual reading energized his imagination. Perhaps I suffer from a little deafness with regard to what Melville heard in Washington Irving. But even if I were to hear it, I wonder what one should say about it. For example, having just read a study of how

32. *The Letters of Herman Melville*, ed. Merrell R. Davis and William H. Gilman (New Haven: Yale University Press, 1960), p. 77.

"Assumption" appears in the story as an extended pun on the legal doctrine of *assumpsit*, I found a critic who said no, it is Melville's "very large pun on the Doctrine of the Assumption, the Catholic belief that the Virgin Mary ascended into Heaven on August 15."[33] I turned to some of the scholarly commentary on the biblical sources for Melville's imagery in "Bartleby" and found one critic suggesting that the dead letters at the end of the story "symbolize the New Testament."[34] Various scenes, details, and lines of dialogue are shown to be Melville's deliberate play with scripture. Matthew 24:27, "For as the lightning cometh out of the east, and shineth even unto the west," is the narrator's "thunderstuck" realization that makes him stand "like the man who, pipe in mouth, was killed one cloudless afternoon long ago in Virginia, by summer lightning." Did Melville steal the lightning, and just add the pipe? Our critic finds another "source" in Matthew 24:16. "Then let him which be in Judea flee into the mountains" is the narrator's, "I answered nothing; but effectually dodging every one by the suddenness and rapidity of my flight, rushed from the building. . . ." The Lawyer does not go all the way from Judea to the mountains, but he does jump on a bus. And, at the end of the story when the grub-man says to the Lawyer, "I thought that friend of yourn was a gentleman forger," we are told to hear the Book of Matthew again: "And many false prophets shall rise, and shall deceive many." Again, the jump from "gentlemen forger" to "false prophets" is a little higher than I want to go. Years ago I read an essay suggesting that in *The Sound and the Fury*, when Jason enters his niece's room on Easter Sunday and finds her underwear strewn about, we should remember

33. Bickley, "'Bartleby' as Paradigm," p. 38.

34. Donald M. Fiene, "Bartleby The Christ," *American Transcendental Quarterly*, 7 (Summer, 1970), 18–23, p. 18.

Jesus's burial cloths after the stone was rolled away from the Tomb. I just could not put that hose and bra on the Son of God. Some critics go right through the Bible to give a local habitation and a name to Christian symbolism: "Bartleby" is about the death of Puritanism, and "Melville forces us to read the narrator's ceaseless interrogation of Bartleby exactly as the Puritan magistrates defended their own inquisition."[35] Note that Melville "forces us" to read "exactly as." My eyes would not do it; they were refusing to read again.

When I went back to Bruce Franklin's seminal essay in *The Wake of the Gods*, I discovered Franklin had found another "source" that may serve here to illustrate the general difficulty we have with any specific instance we find. Franklin proposes that Bartleby is not only Christ, or "the least of these"; he is also a Hindu ascetic, as described in a book Melville knew, Sir Thomas Maurice's *Indian Antiquities*. Franklin asserts that "Bartleby's behavior seems to be the very essence of Maurice's description of the Saniassi's behavior. In fact, Maurice's general description and judgment of the Saniassi often seems to be a precise description and judgment of Bartleby."[36] Initially skeptical of what "in fact" only "often seems to be," I was nevertheless persuaded that several things in Melville's story come from the Reverend Maurice's description of "the systematic withdrawal from the world practiced by the Saniassi." In the fifth stage of that withdrawal, the Saniassi "eats only one particular kind of food during the day and night." At first the Lawyer surmises that Bartleby "must be a vegetarian," but then realizes, "no; he never eats even vegetables, he eats nothing but ginger-

35. Michael Clark, "Witches and Wall Street: Possession Is Nine-Tenths of the Law," *Texas Studies in Language and Literature*, 25 (Spring, 1983), 55–76, p. 65.

36. Franklin, *Wake of the Gods*, pp. 135–36.

nuts." During the final stage, the Saniassi neither eats nor drinks. It is the same with Bartleby. His general demeanor is that of the Saniassi: calm silent, dignified withdrawal from the world, existing solely on charity, making no personal exertion to stay alive. The goal is total indifference to the world, an effort to become as disembodied as a ghost. We are looking carefully at both texts, not away from Melville's, when we say that Bartleby "is" Maurice's Saniassi ascetic: "By long habits of indifference, he becomes inanimate as a piece of wood or stone; and, though he mechanically respires the vital air, he is to all the purposes of active life, *defunct*." What bothers me here is not what bothered me about those allusions I tended to dimiss as too vague or marginal. I do not doubt that Maurice's book was on Melville's mind. My problem is that I do not know what to do with it in mine. My problem, that is, lies with the status of such allusions and identifications. Is any "source" we find supposed to be something the tale comes from, or is it an active effect meant to be seen and understood by the reader? In much of the scholarly and critical commentary this central question goes begging, or it receives what seems to me a wrong answer. Are we saying of whatever we find that it is the "germ" of the tale, a passing fancy, a private joke, a joke Melville meant to share with all of us, or what? Melville might legitimately expect his best readers—not all of them, not even most of them, but the best of them in mid-nineteenth-century America—to hear the biblical allusion when the Lawyer denies Bartleby three times. They may have had to stretch their minds, but they could do it. We may have to have it pointed out to us now, but we can see it. Something altogether different is going on, however, when we see in persuasive detail that Bartleby "is" a Saniassi ascetic. For what contemporary audience or envisioned posterity could Melville present such a figure? Clearly, there can be no question that Melville's mind is eclectic, pedantic, broadly allusive, and sly. In what fabulous chamber of that mind does any "borrowing" sit? Or does it have the run of the place? And what are we to do when we catch a glimpse of it in the hall?

For a long time I have been puzzled by a curious paragraph in "Bartleby" about "the unfortunate Adams and the still more unfortunate Colt." There was a "fatal act": Colt murdered Adams. I asked a colleague about it, and he told me that *C*olt and *A*dams were *C*ain and *A*bel (the paragraph is immediately followed by the narrator's line about the "old Adam of resentment"). I went to the library, where I discovered a helpful article about the Colt-Adams case.[37] It culminated in a sensational murder trial in New York in 1842. The Judge in the Colt-Adams trial called the scene of the crime "the most frequented house in the most populous city in the union: the time midday, and separated only by a folding door was a schoolroom filled with scholars." That is curious, for Melville uses the phrase "solitary office"; he even repeats it, and elaborates it at some length: "being alone in a solitary office, up stairs, of a building entirely unhal-

37. T. H. Giddings, "Melville, the Colt-Adams Murder, and 'Bartleby,'" *Studies in American Fiction*, 2 (Autumn, 1974), 123–32, p. 127. David S. Reynolds discusses both the Colt-Adams case and the case of the famous forger Monroe Edwards in *Beneath the American Renaissance: The Subversive Imagination in the Age of Emerson and Melville* (New York: Knopf, 1988). Reynolds has located yet another source for "Bartleby": the story "might be viewed as a literary version of several of the central images" in George Foster's *New York in Slices* (1849). Foster's "pale young man," Reynolds contends, "seems to directly anticipate Melville's Bartleby" (*sic*). Similarly, Foster's portrait of the Tombs, his brief inventory of items in a pawn shop, and his image of busy Broadway as "a perfect Mississippi" at noon and "some Palmyra avenue" after hours seem to show that Melville found *New York in Slices* richly suggestive. See Reynolds, pp. 295–96.

lowed by humanizing domestic associations—an uncarpeted office, doubtless, of a dusty, haggard sort of appearance;—this it must have been, which greatly helped to enhance the irritable desperation of the hapless Colt." Melville says the opposite of what the judge said. The paragraph sits there, oddly, almost like the "Digression" of a formal argument. Did Melville expect his readers, in 1853, to remember this particular aspect of a scandal over a decade old? Why bring up the "scene of the crime," the most notable feature of which was that it was filled with people, only to say that it was "entirely unhallowed by humanizing domestic associations"? And, if we start playing that game, what on earth does it tell us about "Bartleby"?

Or could it be that we are playing the wrong game? When the Colt-Adams scandal erupted, Melville was at sea on the *Acushnet;* he was in the Galapagos Islands at the time of the actual murder and in Tahiti at the time of the trial. Should we actually go back to the Colt-Adams case because the Lawyer in "Bartleby" mentions it? Has Melville got the details wrong, or has the Lawyer got them wrong? And what do we mean by "wrong"? Do we ask details in a work of fiction to correspond to circumstances in a world quite outside the book? We are not really looking at how the courtroom speech fits into "Bartleby"; we are dragging the fiction of "Bartleby" back to the actual courtroom. We are, quite literally, reading Melville's imagination backward.

Any clearheaded reader can surely hear the echo of *Sartor Resartus,* "all visible things are emblems," in Captain Ahab's declaration to Starbuck that "All visible objects, man, are but as pasteboard masks." When we hear it, we are in no danger of becoming like that Faulkner critic with his hallucination of Jesus lingerie. We know Melville was reading Carlyle, and we can not shut out such persuasive echolalia; the difficulty resides not in what we hear but in how we hear it and what we make of it. One critic says, "Melville felt so uncomfortable over the facile idealism arrived at by Carlyle towards the end of *Sartor Resartus* that he was forced to retaliate by conceiving the character of Ahab."[38] This seems to me the error in much of the "source study" of Melville's reading. If you say Melville got so "uncomfortable" over Carlyle's "facile idealism" (what a way to describe Carlyle!) that he was "forced to retaliate," then you might as well say, as this critic does, that "'I would prefer not to'" becomes "a genteel way of expressing The Everlasting No." Our critic tells us that "Nippers suffers from indigestion—no doubt the Carlylean 'disease of the liver.'" This is like saying "Bartleby" was written out of Melville's rancorous envy of Charles Dickens. We move from clear evidence that Melville was reading Carlyle and Dickens to the claim that he was writing specifically about them. Our critics aren't telling us what Melville read; they are telling us how he read, imputing motives—jealousy and outrage—to him. Melville's mind does not seem largely creative but narrowly peevish. And, I think, the critics do to us something rather like what they do to Melville: in failing to understand how he used his reading they fail to understand how we should read him. Much of the Bartleby Industry is not "source study" at all, finally, for the "source" becomes the subject. Critics claim to have found the "key" to unlock the story. But their metaphor is fundamentally flawed. There is no key. If we have to use a metaphor, perhaps we should think of a jigsaw puzzle rather than a key. Intent on finding the true "source," we fail to show the extent of Melville's wide-ranging indebtedness; we

38. Mario L. D'Avanzo, "Melville's 'Bartleby' and Carlyle," in *Melville Annual 1965, A Symposium: "Bartleby the Scrivener,"* ed. Howard P. Vincent (Kent, Ohio: Kent State University Press, 1966), p. 114.

fail to show how he released himself from his reading and went beyond it to make of it something utterly his own.

Would it not be more sensible to say that he works in his first short story the way he had worked in his six previously published books, copying words and phrases and ideas from other writers, learning from them, transmuting them? It is impossible to understand his actual creative process, in any phase of his career, unless, as Leon Howard suggests, one considers any book he was using "in relation to the literary tradition of which it was a part—that is, unless Melville's own work is examined against the background of works by other writers who were in his mind at the time he planned and wrote his own story."[39] Newton Arvin was correct when he insisted on Melville's "extraordinary dependence on the writings of other men." Melville is unique among his great nineteenth-century contemporaries—Scott, Balzac, Dickens, Dostoevski, Hardy—all of whom Arvin characterizes as "wonderfully originative writers," men who create their "thickly populated worlds out of materials that for the most part are at least once removed from their own personal histories, and that depend only very secondarily on the writings of other men."[40] Melville is quite unlike them. Books are the air he breathes, the oxygen in his blood; he would not be who he is without them. What he writes is not "about" something he read; his work is fueled by all his reading, in large ways and small, intensely empowered by it.

He began as a writer almost accidentally, a young man telling a personal story of his own experience. But even in his first book, *Typee*, he got a little nervous and had to embellish his tale with things from other writers. Beginning with per-

39. Howard, *Herman Melville*, p. 163.

40. Newton Arvin, *Herman Melville* (New York: Viking, 1950), pp. 144–45.

sonal memory, Melville sought support in understanding and expressing his life by going to the library and looking up what other men had said about similar experiences. He sought in their books documentation and verification for his own life. Within three years, however, he was using what he read to inspire and guide him through new worlds of the profoundest spiritual experience. He sawed wood, tended his farm animals, and read everything he could lay his hands on.

The paradoxical achievement of the Bartleby Industry is that any of its single contributions in light of all its others, and the enormous weight of all of them together, can only convince us that there never could have been a "key." Taken whole, the Bartleby Industry persuades us of the truly omnivorous quality of Melville's reading, the uncanny way virtually everything he read stayed with him and found a home somewhere in his magnificently capacious and retentive mind. When he wrote "Bartleby, The Scrivener" he was just entering his thirty-fourth year. Naturally he turned to Dickens, whose *Bleak House* he had just finished. Naturally he dropped in on American neighbors like Emerson. Naturally he turned to the Bible, for he always turned to it, everywhere in his work. He perused the newspapers, with his weak and hurting eyes, and he turned to books that had a vogue in his day but now are virtually forgotten, books such as Maurice's *Indian Antiquities*. He played widely and energetically with all sorts of books. We may quarrel over how important any one of them was to him, but we will never get him right if we fail to see that he read them all and that his genius shattered his reading in the very act of incorporating it.

He was quite serious when, in June of 1851, he wrote to Hawthorne that "what I feel most moved to write, that is banned,—it will not pay. Yet, altogether, write the *other* way

I cannot." How, he wondered, did Shakespeare manage to be both profound and popular? If you have to satisfy the groundlings, how can you satisfy yourself? And when he read Shakespeare, something amazing, something not altogether conscious or voluntary, began happening to him. In *American Renaissance*, still the most valuable book on the period, F. O. Matthiessen concludes that "Melville's imagination instinctively reshaped its impressions to suit his own needs." Shakespeare's

> 'Where a malignant and a turban'd Turk
> Beat a Venetian and traduced the state,'

> is altered to: "No turbaned Turk, no hired Venetian or Malay, could have smote him with more seeming malice." On such levels the borrowed material has entered into the formation of Melville's own thought. . . . The most important effect of Shakespeare's use of language was to give Melville a range of vocabulary for expressing passion far beyond any that he had previously possessed.[41]

Matthiessen's great insight is his realization that "the borrowed material has entered into the formation of Melville's own thought." What is going on is no isolated learned reference, no little allusion; the process unfolding is a profound altering of the mind, for Melville is acquiring a massive old language for a radical new way of seeing the world. Charles Olson apparently misread "sparrows" as "sperms," but he was essentially right about Melville's discovery of Shakespeare, the notes in Melville's hand at the end of his copy of *King Lear*, notes about Pip, Bulkington, Ishmael, and Ahab. Melville's reading and Melville's writing are quite literally there, physically there on the page together, so that meditation and creation become one.

41. F. O. Matthiessen, *American Renaissance: Art and Expression in the Age of Emerson and Whitman* (New York: Oxford University Press, 1941), p. 425.

To be sure, nothing Melville ever read altered his mind so radically as Shakespeare did, unless it was the Bible. But almost anything he read could mean something to him, and even a little story in the newspaper could move him profoundly. His own linguistic resources were marvelously extended and strengthened by his immersion in the Elizabethans; that great experience had the consequence of working in the other direction, too, so that anything he read found itself transformed into the massive instrument of his own language. What had begun in him at least as early as *Mardi* was now second nature to him and a kind of madness: when he sat down to read, he found himself writing. And we should remind ourselves that when he wrote his first short story, he had undergone the crushing experience of writing *Moby-Dick* only to see its commercial defeat; he had suffered through *Pierre* and the unanimous critical disapproval of it. He was exhausted, hurt beyond bearing, by all the heroic work he had done and by the world's rejection of it. But his furious habit of composition continued. Reading anything, the very act of reading itself, had become his central and most powerful generative process. When critics claim too much for a little local source, they fail to deal with the dark awesomeness of his mind. We need to see his use of any one thing not as the key to his imagination but as an example of its deeply obsessive activity. He wrote to Duyckinck, "I love all men who *dive!*" This most powerful of American minds was swimming through libraries, and he happened to kick up all sorts of things in the sand. They intrigued him; he picked them up and turned them over in his "visible hands," way down there, deep down with that "whole corps of thought-divers, that have been diving and coming up again with bloodshot eyes since the world began."

CHAPTER 2

"A Little *Luny*"

"I think, sir, he's a little *luny*," replied Ginger Nut, with a grin.

"I think he is a little deranged," said I, sadly.

Newton Arvin assesses the damage Melville did to himself in writing *Moby-Dick*: he "passed through a prolonged emotional and nervous trial that, at a later period, would promptly have been described as a crack-up, and treated as such." Or, perhaps the "crack-up" was so severe that it could not be healed by any treatment. Arvin notes that "in the months before he had begun the book, and even at times while he was at work on it," Melville struck his family and friends "as still essentially a young man." But then something terrible happened. "After *Moby-Dick* we virtually never have that impression again; already it is a middle-aged man who looks out at us." Melville "had remained young longer than most men, and then when a kind of agedness came, it came swiftly."[1]

I think one should understand the dreadful change in Melville not as some unnatural crack-up but rather as the tragic cost of his labor. How could one write *Moby-Dick* and stay young? *Moby-Dick* is a huge book, and it is huge in a

1. Newton Arvin, *Herman Melville* (New York: Viking, 1950), p. 195.

unique way. Yvor Winters says of it that "probably no other book exists which so impresses us at once with the vastness of the physical universe and with the vastness of the idea of the universe. The allegory is incalculably strengthened by this sense of power, and by the detailed reality through which it is established."

It was back-breaking (we know how Melville complained about his back): he was exploring, as Winters says, "how the idea of the whale is embedded in all nature" and "repeatedly suggested in rocks, in mountains, and stars."[2] Not just a very long book, *Moby-Dick* is an immensely heavy book, often ponderously so—after writing it, how could a man not be damaged for a very long time?

It permanently aged him.

But Melville went ahead, immediately, into the incestuous tortures of *Pierre*. "In the first three years after his removal with his wife and son from New York to 'Arrowhead,'" says Richard Chase, Melville "wrote relentlessly" to the point where it "severely taxed his health"; he seemed "to be writing himself into the ground."[3] More than twenty years later Melville's wife, Lizzie, talks about her husband's writing in the same way she had in the early 1850s. On February 2, 1876, she wrote her cousin Catherine that "if ever this dreadful *incubus* of a book [*Clarel*] (I call it so because it has undermined all our happiness) gets off Herman's shoulders I do hope he may be in better mental health."[4] Some time later she is still worrying "how *morbidly* sensitive" he would always get when he was writing. But the complaint was con-

2. Yvor Winters, *In Defense of Reason* (Denver: Allan Swallow, 1947), p. 213.

3. Richard Chase, *Herman Melville: A Critical Study* (New York: Macmillan, 1949), p. 103.

4. Quoted by Leon Howard in *Herman Melville: A Biography* (Berkeley: University of California Press, 1951), p. 296.

tinuous and long-standing: "We all felt anxious about the strain on his health in the spring of 1853." At the time, Melville's mother, Maria Melville, wrote to Peter Gansevoort that "a change of occupation my dear brother in my opinion is necessary for Herman." Her son's mental state

> would be greatly benefitted by a sojourn abroad, he would then be compelled to more intercourse with his fellow creatures. It would very materially renew, and strengthen both his body and mind. The constant in-door confinement with little intermission to which Herman's occupation as author compels him, does not agree with him. This constant working of the brain, and excitement of the imagination is wearing Herman out. . . .[5]

It must have been an immensely painful ordeal for Melville to go through, and for his family to watch him go through. Melville's father-in-law, Lemuel Shaw, wrote of

> how very ill Herman has been. When he is deeply engaged in one of his literary works, he confines him, [*sic*] to hard study many hours in the day, with little or no exercise, and this specifically in winter for a great many days together. He probably thus overworks himself and brings on severe nervous affections.[6]

Wife, mother, father-in-law, all are saying the same thing. One reason for their sustained efforts to procure a consulship for him is evident—to get the man away from his writing desk. His sciatica and neuralgia were killing him; Dr. Holmes was called in to examine him. To make matters worse—to make them as bad as they really were—his family and friends were whispering about his possible insanity. Those whispers were publicly shouted in all the literary

5. Quoted ibid., p. 204.
6. Quoted ibid., pp. 235–36.

magazines. *Pierre* was unanimously hooted, one critic claiming that "Herman Melville had gone 'clean daft.'" Even *Putnam's* characterized the book as "inexcusable insanity." It was "unnatural," "repulsive," "indecent." Nowhere did it receive a single favorable review. The *Southern Literary Messenger* said the book should be left "unbought on the shelves." George Washington Peck in the *American Whig Review* (November, 1852) said Melville "strikes with an impious, though, happily, weak hand, at the very foundations of society." Even Melville's friend and literary benefactor, Evert Duyckinck, said *Pierre* violated "the most sacred associations of life." If Herman Melville did not drop dead from his work itself, he had ample cause to do so upon reading the reviews of it. What he had created might well have driven any man crazy, and now all about him, both at home and in print, everybody was saying that was just what had happened.

He did not have available to him Nietzsche's assertion that "all worthwhile thought risks madness," but he did have the question of Carlyle's Teufelsdröckh: "Was Luther's Picture of the Devil less a Reality, whether it were formed within the bodily eye, or without it? In every the wisest Soul lies a whole world of internal Madness, an authentic Demon-Empire." In "The Madness of Ahab," Henry Nash Smith points out that "there are intimations in Melville's earlier work, at least from *Mardi* (1849) onward, that insanity can be a means of access to higher truth." When Melville thinks of insanity, he "has in mind an aristocratic distinction between the insight of an elite of deep men and the insensitivity of average mediocrity."[7] In the same year Smith points to, 1849, Melville wrote to Duyckinck about a former editor of the *Literary World*, Charles Fenno Hoffman: "This going

7. Henry Nash Smith, "The Madness of Ahab," *Democracy and the Novel* (New York: Oxford University Press, 1978), 35–55, p. 37.

mad of a friend or acquaintance comes straight home to every man who feels his soul in him . . . and he who has never felt, momentarily, what madness is has but a mouthful of brains."[8]

Moby-Dick and *Pierre* are both, whatever else they are, profound extended treatises on acute intellectual and emotional distress, and they exhausted their author. Again, what else could one expect? What treatment could "fix" it? What therapy could cure Melville's furious composition? His disorientation and despair were the honest wages of heroic work. No wonder when Hawthorne saw him again in Liverpool, he sensed in Melville "a morbid state of mind" and that his old friend had "pretty much made up his mind to be annihilated."[9]

"Bartleby, The Scrivener" was conceived and written in that mental state. Melville saw his own writing environment at Arrowhead as all "paper, pens, and infernally black ink, four leprously dingy white walls, no carpet, a cup of water, and a dry biscuit or two." That description furnishes the law office on Wall Street. Early on in the story the Lawyer thinks Bartleby's eyes are failing him and that this is the reason he has ceased copying. Throughout the early 1850s Melville complains of eye troubles. He wrote, "I only wish that I had more day-time to spend out *in the day;* but like an owl I steal abroad by twilight, owing to the twilight of my eyes." We can see that painful problem in Pierre's eye trouble and his "stealing abroad by twilight." In a more general sense, Newton Arvin is correct in his diagnosis that "it was a reward of Melville's sufferings, given the initial power of his mind,

8. *The Letters of Herman Melville*, ed. Merrell R. Davis and William H. Gilman (New Haven: Yale University Press, 1960), p. 83.

9. See *The English Notebooks of Nathaniel Hawthorne*, ed. Randall Stewart (New York: Modern Language Association of America, 1941), pp. 432–33.

that they enabled him to have glimpses, such as few even of his great contemporaries had, into the murky and chaotic regions of the unconscious."[10] The interplay of psychic damage and creative insight is immensely complicated, and we should see the clarity in the feverishness, the brave sanity in all the dark trouble. One does not minimize Melville's pain to insist on the essential health struggling to master it. Leon Howard notes that Melville's mother and wife and sisters were beginning "to fear that winter that Herman—like his father, during the last weeks of life, before him—was 'peculiar.'" But Howard adds immediately that it is also true that "the son was experiencing the excitement of creation rather than of desperation."[11]

Rather than opposing one to the other, might we not say that Melville was profoundly experiencing both? His neighbor, Mrs. Morewood, learned that he would become "engaged in a new work as frequently not to leave his room till quite dark in the evening," and she told him he "must therefore write under a state of morbid excitement which will soon injure his health"—to which Melville cheerfully replied that he was "slightly insane." We should not accept altogether wholeheartedly the verdict of Melville's contemporaries or the characterizations of him by so many critics since. The man was half-dead with overwork and disappointment at its meager reward. But look at the finished work, and look at the work in progress. Melville was thirty-three when he wrote "Bartleby"; we should not retroactively burden him with his long and tragic life. The work he was doing in 1853 issued in *The Piazza Tales*, receiving excellent reviews. Leon Howard notes that Melville's first try at magazine fiction was "embarrassingly successful" and that "the public reception of 'Bar-

10. Arvin, *Herman Melville*, p. 222.
11. Howard, *Herman Melville*, p. 173.

tleby' seems to have been almost wholly favorable."[12] Melville was once again returning from disaster—as, a few years before, after being soundly derided for *Mardi*, he bounced back with *Redburn* and *White Jacket*. The *New York Evening Post* welcomed the recovery of the author of *Typee* and *Omoo* "from that uneasy sleep, during which his genius was disturbed by such distempered dreams as *Mardi*, and frightful nightmares like the ambiguous *Pierre*."[13] In his letters to Hawthorne written right before "Bartleby," Melville shows himself to be a young man powerfully jumping into an idea for a story and totally involved with it imaginatively; what speaks clearly in those letters is a burning desire to write.

In "Bartleby" we see, to be sure, an "innate and incurable disorder" at the very center of things. Ginger Nut says only one line in the story, and it is a beauty: "I think, sir, he's a little *luny*." The Lawyer repeats that line, in his own words, at the end: "I think he is a little deranged." Yes, there is clearly something morbid about poor Bartleby. But, just as clearly, there is nothing morbid about "Bartleby, The Scrivener." Melville's is a tragic imagination, and perhaps one cannot have such an imagination without terrible consequences. But in his short story we do not find our author saying "I prefer not to" to life. Something catastrophically painful was surely going on, but Melville the artist, was going on radiantly. It is a pity that scholars have put so much effort into asking us to choose between Melville sick and Melville sound; everything we know about him compels us to conclude that both stories—and only both of them together—are true.

Mrs. Morewood was very concerned that her neighbor would often write all day long without taking in any solid

12. Ibid., p. 211.
13. Ibid.

food. In the only two pieces Melville published in 1853, "Bartleby" and "Cock-A-Doodle-Do!" the culminating point is death by starvation. Leon Howard says of Merrymusk in "Cock-A-Doodle-Do!": "Like Bartleby, he would not gabble; and also like Bartleby, he and his family with him died in a state of pallid malnutrition."[14] Newton Arvin cannot be far wrong when he asserts that "in fantasy" Melville "allowed himself to die of sheer hunger like Bartleby."[15] We can see why readers have difficulty restraining themselves when they modernize Melville's imagination and compare it to Kafka's "The Hunger Artist," in which they find an echo of the Lawyer's conversations with Bartleby:

> "I have to fast, I can't help it," said the hunger artist. "What a fellow you are," said the overseer, "and why can't you help it?"

Allan F. Stein calls our attention to the names of the three regular employees: they are *food*, Turkey, Nippers (lobster claws), and Ginger Nut.[16] Food and drink rule all three of them. There is considerable byplay involving sending out for food, there is much talk of indigestion, and Bartleby is characterized by the food he eats—that is, as the opposite of it, for he is not "hot and spicy." The Lawyer tries to understand Bartleby on the basis of what he first understands as a vegetarian diet, and thinks of Bartleby's initial industry in terms of eating: "as if long famishing . . . he seemed to gorge himself," with "no pause for digestion." One hears it everywhere, in the little moral menu of a "delicious" "sweet morsel," in the "grub-man," who is described as a "meat-like

14. Ibid., p. 209.
15. Arvin, *Herman Melville*, p. 211.
16. Allan F. Stein, "The Motif of Voracity in 'Bartleby,'" *Emerson Society Quarterly*, 21 (1975), 29–34.

man," and in the final pages, where Bartleby "eats nor hungers any more" and at last "lives without dining."

"Bartleby," then, is a particularly resonant instance of a concern we find all through Melville's writing, one that appears so persistently and with such prominence that it constitutes a major theme of his work. For all his talk about free sexuality in *Typee*, young Herman Melville spends a great deal of his time sitting around joyously eating. Leon Howard reminds us that "of all their customs that Melville wrote of later, he described most precisely without the help of other authorities those dealing with the preparation of food."[17] Throughout his books Melville frequently sees the world in terms of "appetite"—the Cook's marvelous comic sermon in *Moby-Dick* on "woraciousness" and Ishmael's cry, "Oh, horrible vulturism of earth from which not the mightiest whale is free." At the end of his life, in "Billy Budd," the idea of vulturism is orchestrated in terror. Richard Chase has noted "the large number of figures of speech having to do with the act of eating."[18] In the very first encounter, "plump upon Billy at first sight in the gangway the boarding officer Lieutenant Ratcliffe pounced"; to get him like "a goldfinch popped into a cage," the officer sits "settling himself in his seat and smacking his lips." The ultimate fear about eating, that is, fear of cannibalism, expressed in his first book, is everywhere in the action and language of the last book. Captain Graveling says the crew fell for Billy, and "they took to him like hornets to treacle." The big fellow, Red Whiskers, "under pretence of showing Billy just whence a sirloin steak was cut—for the fellow had once been a butcher—insultingly gave him a dig under the ribs." And Claggart's

17. Howard, *Herman Melville*, p. 52.

18. Richard Chase, "Introduction," in *Selected Tales and Poems by Herman Melville* (New York: Holt, Rinehart, Winston, 1960), p. xiv.

"mesmeric glance" at Billy is "the hungry lurch of the torpedo-fish." This, with a deadly vengeance, is the "horrible vulturism of earth."

It is the dark underside of what Melville frequently presents with comic gusto. Edwin Haviland Miller maintains that "unencumbered or manic delight in Melville's writing is associated with feasting, usually in an all-male society"; "in his fictions the orgies are oral Edens."[19] The language of Miller's formulation points to the clear substitution of eating for sexuality, a substitution that was clear to Melville himself, for he often has a good deal of fun with it. He usually insists that these oral Edens take place before the Fall, or instead of it. In his story "The Paradise of Bachelors," the men's joy depends directly on their having "no wives, or children to give an anxious thought" to their feasting, and their celibate revels are so intense that "little have you seen, just nothing do you know, not the sweet kernel have you tasted, till you dine among the banded Bachelors, and see their convivial eyes and glasses sparkle." Melville pulls himself up into elaborate mock-heroics, comparing "glorious battling for the Holy Land" to "the carving of roast mutton at a dinner-board" and wondering, "Do these degenerate Templars now think it sweeter far to fall in banquet than in war?" It is a bloody campaign, an engagement *au jus*, "led by that well-known English generalissimo, roast beef" with "a fat turkey, a chicken-pie, and endless other savory things" as "aides-de-camp," and a "picked brigade of game-fowl encamped upon the board, their camp-fires lit by the ruddiest of decanters." Melville's heroic similes run away with him, for this is a fantasia of the "solid food" he could not eat while writing it. The manic delight spills into puns: as Bruce

19. Edwin Haviland Miller, *Melville* (New York: George Braziller, 1975), p. 263.

Franklin notes, the "Temple Bar" itself "is an anus," and the narrator turns, "soiled with the mud of Fleet Street," and glides "down a dim, monastic way, flanked by dark, sedate, and solemn piles" (*sic*) to begin with "ox-tail soup."[20]

Part of the grim fun lies in the way this anal world is immediately contrasted to the brutal genital world of the companion piece, "The Tartarus of Maids." There is the horrible first paragraph of penetration with its "odorous grasses," wherein "you enter ascendingly among bleak hills" and "cloven walls" past the "crazy spinster's hut having long ago stood somewhere hereabouts." Melville obsessively pursues his terrible joke about "the sudden contraction of the gorge" and the "great purple, hopper-shaped hollow" and the "turbid brick-colored stream" of "Blood River" in this "Mad Maid's Bellows-pipe." One cannot help wondering how in the world Melville's contemporary polite readership took all this "seedsman's business"—that "strange, blood-like, abdominal heat" of the room where the "germinous particles" are deposits from "two great round vats," the ovaries "full of a white, wet, wooly-looking stuff not unlike the albuminous part of an egg, soft-boiled." This ghastly mischief started with that "vertical thing like a piston periodically rising and falling." Cupid tells us that the finished product comes out in "nine minutes." This is no lusty Rabelaisian outburst; it is a nightmare vision of sexuality in terms of enslavement and brutality. The narrator says that "what made the thing I saw so specially terrible to me was the metallic necessity, the unbudging fatality which governed it." And he interrupts the awful allegory to ask, "But where are the gay bachelors?" He concludes by explicitly linking

20. Bruce Franklin, "Herman Melville: Artist of the Worker's World," in *Weapons of Criticism: Marxism in America and the Literary Tradition*, ed. Norman Rudich, (Palo Alto, Calif.: Ramparts, 1976), pp. 298–99.

them in the last line: "All alone with inscrutable nature, I exclaimed—Oh! Paradise of Bachelors! and oh! Tartarus of Maids!" The world of food and the world of sex are fatally opposed; the first is all joyous abundance and the second all tortured bareness, deprivation, and cruelty.

In "Bartleby" the substitution of food for sex works in rather a different way. Some critics see more sexual imagery in it than I do: one reader insists on the "phallic, in the comic erections of self (i.e., when Turkey is up and Nippurs is down)"—and perhaps that error, "Nipp*urs*," is not unconnected to seeing the poor guy this way.[21] Another reader sees the story as "a classic case of depression," displaying "overtones of homosexuality."[22] We may not quite agree on the exact nature of the sexuality here, but we know that Melville had already written "A Squeeze of the Hand" and "The Cassock" in *Moby-Dick*, and soon he would make all those jokes about "a big cock" in "Cock-A-Doodle-Do!," elaborate all those puns in "The Tartarus of Maids," and finally compose that immensely painful "Digression" on ejaculation in "Billy Budd." It would not be untoward to assume that there is a sexual dimension to "No.—Wall Street."

One way of looking at it is suggested by Patricia Barber in her essay "What If Bartleby Were a Woman?" Barber right away says her question is an "impossible joke," and then she shows us that it is a serious one, too, for it points to an essential mystery in the story.[23] Barber says the gender

21. Christopher Bollas, "Melville's Lost Self: *Bartleby*," *American Imago*, 31 (Winter, 1974), 401–11, p. 402.

22. George Bluestone, quoted in *Melville Annual 1965, A Symposium: "Bartleby the Scrivener,"* ed. Howard P. Vincent (Kent, Ohio: Kent State University Press, 1966), p. 49.

23. Patricia Barber, "What If Bartleby Were a Woman?," in *The Authority of Experience: Essays in Feminist Criticism*, ed. Arlyn Diamond and Lee R. Edwards (Amherst: University of Massachusetts Press, 1977), p. 219.

change is a modest exercise: "to 'write' Miss Bartleby's story I have done no more to Melville's version than change 'man' to 'woman' or 'lady,' alter the pronouns and keep everything else the same." Then she briefly tells the story, and discovers that "one of the most striking aspects about the sex-changed story is how gracefully it works," for it remains a story "about affluent complacency shaken by passive, irrational refusal." "By the nature of his mysterious ailment," Bartleby is "so devitalized, so unerotic, that he becomes for us essentially sexless."[24] I want to come back to that phrase, "the nature of his mysterious ailment," but Barber points out that "the frequent use of juristical terms" is the Lawyer's linguistic defense "against the depth and intensity of his feelings for Bartleby, and it is essentially a love story, a story about a man who is confined in an office setting that forbids intimacy and who comes to love a person he cannot save." One would think that in the scene when Bartleby is discovered in "dishabille," the sex change would radically alter not only Bartleby but the Lawyer's response to "her." This obviously erotic element seems foreign to the real story. We have to make quite a shift when we read the narrator's offer to take Miss Bartleby home with him. If Bartleby is a woman, the narrator might feel "impotent," might feel that her refusal "not only disarmed me, but unmanned me." But, of course, that is exactly what the Lawyer does feel—"impotent" and "unmanned"—with Bartleby himself.

Whenever I teach *Moby-Dick* I ask the young women in the class what it is like for them—truly, what is it like, as a woman, to read the book? I was stopped in my tracks by a young woman who took objection to my paraphrasing Charles Olson's claim that this great epic story of carnage and slaughter is "what moves us as a people." She wrote me a

24. Ibid.

note: "All that killing is not what moves *us* as a people—it's what moves *men* as a people." Her point was well taken, I thought, and we talked about the anguished colloquy in "The Symphony" between Ahab and Starbuck about "wife and child" when "the pensive air" is "transparently pure and soft, with a woman's look." Melville opposes that "feminine air" to the "troubled, murderous thinkings of the masculine sea." Such passages illustrate the deep sexual agony Melville frequently tells us is fueling Ahab's mad chase. Shortly before the *Pequod* sails there is a rumor that the Captain "has been found one night lying prone upon the ground, and insensible" because "his ivory limb having been so violent displaced, that it had stake-wise smitten, and all but pierced his groin."

There are traces of that "agonizing wound" in "Bartleby." The story, in its own quiet way, is as clearly a tale of men without women as is the great phallic fury of *Moby-Dick*. In the novel, women are only talked about; they do not receive even that status in "Bartleby." The narrator mentions a cleaning lady who has one key to the office. The only other reference, which Melville later deleted, was the grub-man's wife, "Mrs. Cutlets," and a possible dinner in her "private room." As I have said, I think Melville was right to excise her from the end of the story and to cut the line about the availability of her "private room." Bartleby is too far gone—the story itself has gone too far; any hint of getting out of the tragedy, even to the brief comfort of a private room, would be inappropriate in the end game. We can see just how jarring it would be when we look at Walter Aschaffenburg's opera version of "Bartleby": after the Lawyer painfully moves away from Bartleby's "I know where I am":

> Just then, from the side of the forestage, a huge woman approaches the Lawyer. Her name is Mrs. Cutlets and she is the

grubwoman of the establishment. You will note that there was no special reason to write this role for a man as Melville suggests in the story. It was a natural switch of the sexes and gave me still another opportunity to achieve variety in vocal color. Mrs. Cutlets, a Contralto, must be broadly played for comic relief.[25]

Note that despite what Melville "suggests," "no special reason" inhibits "a natural switch of the sexes" when we seek "variety in vocal color" and "comic relief." This grotesque idea of a "huge woman" is helpful by negative example, for there are no mothers, no wives, no sisters, no sweethearts in "Bartleby." Ginger Nut is just a boy, but one wonders if the violent passions of Turkey and Nippers would be that way if there were women in their lives. Or, as a student said to me, "the Lawyer couldn't invite Bartleby to go home with him if he had a wife—or at least wouldn't he have to ask her?" "A Story of Wall Street" is full of food, and there is not a woman in it. This is "The Tartarus of Bachelors." It is not a question of food, or sex, or food instead of sex; all appetite has atrophied, and whatever has hurt Bartleby has hurt him utterly.

A frequent "explanation" of Bartleby is that he is schizophrenic. George Bluestone calls it "catatonic schizophrenia."[26] Newton Arvin suggests that "there is a level on which 'Bartleby' can be described as a wonderfully intuitive study in what would now be called schizophrenia, and in Melville himself there were certainly the germs of schizophrenic detachment."[27]

But another reader complains that we "have mistakenly called Bartleby schizophrenic," for he is suffering from quite

25. Walter Aschaffenburg, quoted in *Melville Annual 1965*, ed. Vincent, p. 40.

26. George Bluestone, quoted in *Melville Annual 1965*, ed. Vincent, p. 49.

27. Arvin, *Herman Melville*, p. 243.

a different kind of mental illness. Those whom this illness strikes "appear to be without the delusions or hallucinations that attend schizophrenia." Instead, "they may sit for hours, immobile, gazing reflectively into space. When left to themselves, as in merely custodial institutions, they are liable to vegetate." The disease cannot be cured, but it can be controlled; a sufferer can hold down a job as "bank teller, laboratory technician, accountant, and duplicating machine operator." Their parents say that these people live "like in a shell" and are "happiest when left alone." They "give the impression of silent wisdom." Moreover, "the meaning of a word becomes inflexible and cannot be used with any but the originally acquired connotation." They "learn stock phrases as though they were single words." Physical behavior imitates linguistic behavior, for the victim's "noises and motions and all of his performances are as monotonously repetitious as are his verbal utterances." Frequently, there is "the refusal of food."

The descriptions I have quoted here are remarkably characteristic of Bartleby. But none of them was said with Bartleby in mind. These are descriptions, by their doctors and relatives, of autistic children. Their stories are gathered together by William P. Sullivan in his amazing article "Bartleby and Infantile Autism: A Naturalistic Explanation," in *The Bulletin of the West Virginia Association of College English Teachers*, 3, no. 2 (Fall, 1976), 43–60. I document it here in my text because it is so hard to come by (it is miscited in the *PMLA* Annual Bibliography). Sullivan begins by saying we can never hope to explain Bartleby, for how can one explain "the mystery of the inner life of a man who seems as remote as a star?" But that very mystery prompts us to try to find a theory. The word *autism* was first used by Eugen Bleuler in 1911; the first American to explore it, in 1943, was Leo

Kanner. In the psychiatric commentary of Henry A. Murray it is now actually called "the Bartleby complex." Freud said, at his seventieth birthday dinner, that he had not claimed to "invent" or "discover" the psychiatric concepts he was using—he was only trying to systematize what poets had seen centuries before. That is why he used "the Oedipus complex." So might it not make good sense to speak of the "Bartleby complex"? The Lawyer says that maybe his intervention is hopeless, if Bartleby is the victim of "innate and incurable disorder." Sullivan quotes a similar conclusion by a psychiatrist who worked with autistic children: "Little spirit of therapeutic hopefulness attends this work because, by all reports, this is an incurable illness no matter what the intervention."

Throughout the story, Sullivan says, Bartleby seems to suffer from the phenomenon of "double audition" that autistic persons experience: they hear things twice, and one must wait a long time for them to answer a question because they have to sort out the words. Often when speaking to Bartleby, as the Lawyer tells us at the end of the story, he has to wait "a considerable time for a reply." Autistics avoid eye contact (Bartleby keeps his eyes on the bust of Cicero as he talks with the Lawyer); autistics avoid group activities (Bartleby refuses to join the other scriveners to compare copies). Autistic persons "learn stock phrases as though they were single words," repeating phrases over and over (an extraordinarily high percentage of Bartleby's utterances are only slight variations on that single repetitive phrase, "I prefer not to"). Throughout the story, Sullivan points out, Bartleby has "difficulty with communication." At the very end of the story, when Bartleby lies dead, the Lawyer does the one thing that might have worked when Bartleby was alive—"Something prompted me to touch him. I felt his hand. . . ."

Sullivan notes that "in dealing with autistic children, first encounters should be tactile, rather than visual or auditory." The Lawyer should not have invited Bartleby to come home with him; he should have taken Bartleby by the hand and led him there.

I don't see how anyone can read Sullivan's essay without seeing Bartleby, time and time again. But does Bartleby have "difficulty with communication"? It is the Lawyer who has difficulty with communication. Bartleby is certainly not an easy person to deal with, and there is no real answer to what he says, but he does not seem to have any trouble saying it. Autism is a severe neurological disorder; something seems to have been badly disturbed in the brain's filter system, and only half its victims develop any speech at all. We have no evidence, no matter how carefully we read what he says and does, that Bartleby's brain is damaged. His soul, yes. The Lawyer says "soul." To see Bartleby's trouble as a chemical malfunction of the brain is contradicted by his actual behavior. When we study the actual lines Bartleby speaks, we have to notice that a certain obdurate wit springs up naturally in the special delicacy of his phrasing. Bartleby is thinking twice, not hearing double.

There is something shrewd and cool and exasperating about him. The Lawyer is not unkind to see that whatever disorder may be present, there seems "to lurk in it a certain calm disdain." Bartleby is clearly the victim of something, and the Lawyer realizes it, and as we read the story, we realize it, too. But Bartleby is very knowing, time after time. The problem is not that Bartleby's brain does not work; the problem is that Bartleby will not work. What he says, not how he says it, is difficult to contend with; he displays no impairment of speech, no stutter or groping for words. Quite the contrary: "Not a wrinkle of agitation rippled him."

The idea of schizophrenia depends on how one defines it. In his essay "Bartleby and Schizophrenia," Morris Beja cites a case study of a schizophrenic from the *British Journal of Medical Psychology*. It is uncanny in its relation to Bartleby: a young man, "compulsively prone to repetitive phrases," "began to stop and stand still," and finally "would each day stand rigidly in the same spot for periods varying from one to three hours" and would "look at this blank wall." His behavior exhibited "a general slowing up and impairment in efficiency in carrying out all his usual activities." Beja is right to say that however we may speak of "echolalia" or "flexibilitas cerea (inert flexibility)" we must see that "Bartleby's words suggest that his behavior is a volitional response to his situation, consciously—even provocatively—made."[28] Beja cites the work of R. D. Laing, especially Laing's distinction between "break-down" and "break-through," to show us that mental and emotional aberration is often a genuine response of a sensitive mind to an intolerable situation. This is what Melville so frequently says—seeing the world clearly, for the monstrous place it is, is what drives one mad.

I am astonished at the frequent critical assertion that the Lawyer's understanding Bartleby as the victim of "innate and incurable disorder" reveals his failure to take responsibility for Bartleby and care for him. To see someone you love going crazy does not mean you stop loving him. Beja says that "only an inordinately cynical reading of Melville's story will fail to recognize that the lawyer does come to experience genuine love for the scrivener."[29] There is quite a story between the Lawyer's initial failure to see "any thing ordinarily human" about Bartleby and his final cry "Ah Bar-

28. Morris Beja, "Bartleby and Schizophrenia," *Massachusetts Review*, 19 (1978), 555–68, p. 561.

29. Ibid., p. 568.

tleby! Ah humanity!" Bartleby is not "autistic" or "schizophrenic." But something is killing him—something does kill him. Slowly, carefully, he refuses food. And finally he dies. He starves to death. Sometimes we call such a man a martyr. But a martyr is usually rather careful to tell us why, to tell us that some great wrong in the world has forced him to this special act of extreme defiance. When you ask Bartleby to tell you why, he answers, "I prefer not to." He goes to his grave saying it.

It has been suggested that actual men, some of whom Melville knew personally, were models for Bartleby. George J. Adler, with whom Melville enjoyed talking metaphysics, developed severe agoraphobia and had to be confined to an asylum. Another man, Eli James Murdock Fly, whom Melville knew from boyhood, wrote incessantly from morning to night and became a confirmed invalid. And, in Abram C. Dayton's *Last Days of Knickerbocker Life in New York* (1897), Allan Emery has discovered

> two well-known lunatics who frequented the streets of New York City in the 1830s and who seem to have been, in some measure, the real-life counterparts of Bartleby. One of them, McDonald Clarke, was an individual "harmless and inoffensive in manner," who "lounged about the street, assuming an abstracted air, with his gaze fixed upon the pavement as if weighed down by some poignant sorrow." Clarke, like Bartleby, was eventually sent to the Tombs. The other, nick-named "The Gingerbread Man," aimlessly hurried up and down the streets, had no known relatives, acquaintances, occupation, or place of residence, and relied upon gingerbread as his "only visible article of diet." Superimposing these two eccentrics produces a peculiarly accurate approximation of Bartleby.[30]

Melville may have used any—or all—of these men.

30. Allan Emery, "The Alternatives of Melville's 'Bartleby,'" *Nineteenth-Century Fiction*, 31 (1976), 170–87, p. 178, n. 14.

What is not conjectural is Melville's extensive use of the psychological theory of his own time. We hear it in the precise language about Ahab's madness being "subject to his perceptibility, not to his will determinate." In several places Melville is using the 1844 decision *Commonwealth* v. *Rogers*, written by his father-in-law, Lemuel Shaw. In an attempt to extend the insanity defense, Shaw went beyond the famous *McNaughton* decision of the previous year: even if the monomaniac can distinguish right from wrong he cannot help doing wrong. The monomaniac's mind "broods over *one idea* and cannot be reasoned out of it." Melville uses the word *monomaniac* several times, in the way Shaw defined it. Melville says that "if such a furious trope may stand," Ahab's "special lunacy stormed his general sanity." Ishmael/Melville cries out, "God help thee, old man, thy thoughts have created a creature in thee." The relationship between "external shocks" and "moral shocks" is intensely subtle, and one must not assume that the mind "breaks" like a leg. Melville says of Ahab that "it is not probable that this monomania in him took its instant rise at the precise time of his bodily dismemberment." What The Whale does to Ahab is, in one sense, what the Dead Letter Office does to Bartleby—it focuses, it provides an overwhelming instance of something already experienced, it pushes the man off the cliff into the abyss he had already been staring at. Melville says Ahab was "deliriously transferring" a sense of universal evil to the white whale. Henry Nash Smith says that "since Robert Burton's *Anatomy of Melancholy* (1621), 'delirium' had referred to the cognitive errors of the insane." It was also much in Lemuel Shaw's mind as he addressed himself to monomania as "*manie sans délire*."[31]

The most interesting thing here is neither the actual men

31. Smith, "The Madness of Ahab," p. 42.

who might have been role models for Bartleby nor the use of contemporary writings on insanity. Melville had available to him a language for mental disorder that was still fatally confused with clumsy notions of the mind as a storebox of "faculties." In his finest insights Melville breaks free of that language into a peculiarly modern notion of the mind. He penetrates into what we now call "the unconscious." In *Moby-Dick* he takes us on a little tour down "far beneath the fantastic towers of man's upper earth" to the baths buried beneath the Hôtel de Cluny in Paris. Professor Smith sees "the most cryptic metaphor in the book" in the mythic figures of Kronos-Saturn and Zeus-Jupiter, the allegorical embodiments Melville inherited, the myth that provides imaginative access to the insight. In a larger sense, however, it is not cryptic at all. In language of astonishing power, we see Melville hold up in his hands the great bleeding heart of his book: Ahab's

> root of grandeur, his whole awful essence sits in bearded state; an antique buried beneath antiquities, and throned on torsoes! So with a broken throne, the great gods mock that captive king; so like a Caryatid, he patient sits, upholding on his frozen brow the piled entablatures of ages. Wind ye down there, ye prouder, sadder souls! question that proud, sad king! A family likeness! aye, he did beget ye, ye young exiled royalties; and from your grim sire only will the old State-secret come.

This is the human mind itself, "all mutilated." It is a ferocious anatomy of Western culture in general and Captain Ahab in particular, the piled "entablatures of ages" upheld on a "frozen brow." Here is what breaks the heart and freezes the blood: "all that most maddens and torments; all that stirs up the lees of things; all truth with malice in it; all that cracks the sinews and cakes the brain; all the subtle demonisms of life and thought."

Perhaps I can clarify my idea by way of something a

graduate student said to me about the ending of *Moby-Dick*. When the white whale attacks the *Pequod*, Melville is building on the celebrated case in Owen Chase's narrative of the *Essex "Attacked and Finally Destroyed by a Large Spermacetti-Whale."* But Melville inserts an extraordinary detail that one cannot find in Chase's story. It begins with "a low rumbling sound," a kind of "subterraneous hum," which brings the crew to the rail, "all their enchanted eyes intent upon the whale." Moby-Dick has at them: "from side to side strangely vibrating his predestined head," sending "a broad band of over-spreading semicircular foam before him as he rushed." My graduate student had come home to literature after two years of scientific work at the Scripps' Oceanographic Institute in La Jolla, California; he said that what Melville is describing here, long before our science discovered it, is sonar. A sperm whale's sonar, at full power, can violently churn the water into a band of "semicircular foam" by the motion of its "side to side strangely vibrating" head, fixing its equipment with that "low rumbling" and "subterraneous hum." Herman Melville, said my graduate student, "didn't know '*sonar*,' '*so*und *na*vigation *r*anging,'" but he had described its operation with uncanny accuracy.

We say that Moby Dick is a "symbol." Everybody knows that, probably knows it too well. But Melville never calls it a "symbol"; he calls it "allegory." "Symbolism," as Newton Arvin reminds us, did not come into use, not in the sense we use today, until some twenty years after *Moby-Dick* was written. The most famous symbol in American Literature predates symbolism. The Whale's "sonar" is Bartleby the scrivener's "autism" or "schizophrenia" or "mental illness."

The Lawyer knows something is wrong with Bartleby. Those critics who read what the Lawyer says as an unwitting comment on himself are not listening to how accurate his comments are:

So true it is, and so terrible too, that up to a certain point the thought or sight of misery enlists our best affections; but, in certain special cases, beyond that point it does not. They err who would assert that invariably this is owing to the inherent selfishness of the human heart. It rather proceeds from a certain hopelessness of remedying excessive and organic ill. To a sensitive being, pity is not seldom pain. And when at last it is perceived that such pity cannot lead to effectual succor, common sense bids the soul be rid of it. What I saw that morning persuaded me that the scrivener was the victim of innate and incurable disorder. I might give alms to his body; but his body did not pain him; it was his soul that suffered, and his soul I could not reach.

Many critics say the Lawyer's denial that he belongs to those who suffer from "the inherent selfishness of the human heart" actually shows that he is the perfect example of it. Indeed, the critics note, the Lawyer proudly groups himself with another class of people, the elite, for he is a "sensitive being." Such a reading seems to me perverse. The Lawyer's diction and cadences will not support it. Critics read the passage as a rather too fond farewell, as if "his soul I could not reach" means that the Lawyer quits. But the man immediately contradicts by his action what he has just concluded. He reaches for that soul. And he does a very smart thing: saying to himself that he may not be able to do it, that he may lack what he needs to reach an adequate understanding, he resolves to suggest to Bartleby that he "return to his native place, wherever that might be." You must go "home," and I will help pay for your trip. If being with your family restores you, a letter from you will "be sure of a reply."

"Will you tell me, Bartleby, where you were born?"

"I would prefer not to."

"Will you tell me *any thing* about yourself?"

"I would prefer not to."

These questions quite properly involve the past and family, the possible origin of this "incurable disorder"; they point in the right direction to where a possible "cure" might be found after all. The questions produce the only instance in the story when Bartleby has trouble articulating words: "there was the faintest conceivable tremor of the white attenuated mouth." It is too close to home. The very next thing the Lawyer says is "Bartleby, never mind then about revealing your history." What the critics see as a stiff refusal and abandonment is actually a delicate little drama. The Lawyer thinks it over:

> If he would but have named a single relative or friend, I would instantly have written, and urged their taking the poor fellow away to some convenient retreat. But he seemed alone, absolutely alone in the universe.

I see no good reason to doubt—and several very good reasons to believe—that the Lawyer "would instantly have written." Bartleby is one of those "special cases" of "misery" which produce in us "a certain hopelessness of remedying excessive and organic ill." Critics say the Lawyer is too full of easy pity. It is the Lawyer himself who says that "pity cannot lead to effectual succor."

But I wonder if "mental illness" is really any better than specific characterizations such as autism, schizophrenia, or even old "melancholy adust." John Haag, an actor who played Bartleby in a movie version of the story, has said that if he were to list "the most important qualities of the character as I came to know him . . . I think I would commence with Dignity. Bartleby's personal dignity never falters before the world."[32] "Never falters" reminds us of Bartleby's

32. Quoted by William P. Sullivan, "Bartleby and Infantile Autism: A

extraordinary strength and poise. As Maurice Friedman points out, the Lawyer "oscillates between seeing Bartleby as a free and voluntary agent and as a helpless victim of an incurable disorder because he cannot get him into steady focus the one way or the other."[33] Leo Marx asks us what the Lawyer asks himself, "Is it possible that Bartleby's suffering is, to some extent, self-inflicted?"[34] That quality is everywhere in the story, too. It balances all the assertions about "organic ill" and "incurable disorder." Neither assessment of Bartleby is adequate without the other. Moreover, we may be fooling ourselves to think that once we label something, we understand it. Henry Nash Smith concludes of Ahab's madness that "doctors may speak of the surprising powers of reasoning to be observed in some monomaniacs, may even demonstrate that Hamlet and Lear are textbook cases, but this clinical approach cannot possibly do justice to the grandeur that Melville sees in such tragic protagonists, and wishes to confer on Ahab."[35] I am reminded of a colleague's comment to me about the wild goose chase of Conrad critics who try to explain the phrase "unspeakable rites" in *Heart of Darkness*. All those articles "proving" the rites to be sexual orgies, or cannibalism, or whatever else the critics may think of as "unspeakable," only make the rites "speakable." But, by definition, they are "unspeakable." Similarly, with Bartleby: when we ask what is wrong with him, Bartleby will not tell us, the Lawyer cannot tell us, and the story itself does not tell us. It is enigmatic at the core. The repeated answer to our question, and the profoundest, is silence.

Naturalistic Explanation," *Bulletin of the West Virginia Association of College English Teachers*, 3, no. 2 (Fall, 1976), 43–60, p. 56.

33. Maurice Friedman, quoted in *Melville Annual 1965*, ed. Vincent, p. 80.

34. Leo Marx, "Melville's Parable of the Walls," *Sewanee*, 61 (1953), 602–27, p. 618.

35. Smith, "The Madness of Ahab," p. 43.

CHAPTER 3

"A Passive Resistance"

"Nothing so aggravates an earnest person as a passive resistance."

Many critics read "Bartleby" in political terms. Michael Rogin asserts, in *Subversive Genealogy: The Politics and Art of Herman Melville*, that "Bartleby protests, with 'passive resistance,' against his condition. In refusing to copy, he is copying Thoreau. 'I simply wish to refuse allegiance,' announced Thoreau, 'to withdraw.' Bartleby's 'I prefer not to' is an echo of 'Civil Disobedience.'"[1] Rogin goes on to say that "the intent of passive resistance was to save the adversary as well as to triumph over him." Rogin reminds us that Thoreau's father was weak and his brother dead, just as "Melville had a weak, dead father." Thoreau and Melville both chose a "nonviolent form of rebellion," and stepped back from "straightforward, aggressive triumphs."[2] Rogin's conflations seem to me wrongheaded, and the trouble starts, I think, with "passive resistance."

The idea, so frequently expressed, is that "Bartleby himself strikingly foreshadows Mahatma Gandhi's awesome

1. Michael Rogin, *Subversive Genealogy: The Politics and Art of Herman Melville* (Berkeley: University of California Press, 1985), p. 195.

2. Ibid., p. 195.

philosophy of passive resistance."[3] Another critic says: "Thoreau's passive resistance" (note that it is no longer Bartleby's—now it *is* Thoreau's) places Bartleby in a line "from Socrates to Gandhi."[4] Another speaks of "passive resistance" as "that phrase we so associate with Thoreau."[5]

While readers may associate "passive resistance" with Thoreau, the phrase never appears in Thoreau's writing. The Lawyer in "Bartleby" says, "Nothing so aggravates an earnest person as *a* passive resistance" (emphasis mine). That "a" puts the two words in a context rather different from the one today's critics reflexively use. "A passive resistance," in the Lawyer's remarks, isn't "Passive Resistance," a phrase in general circulation. I have been unable to find "passive resistance" anywhere in nineteenth-century America. Maybe it is somewhere, and someone may find it or already has; one would expect to find it in Garrison or Tappan or Theodore Weld or Angelina Grimké or Henry C. Wright, but the closest I came was "nonresistance" and "nonviolent resistance." After John Brown, in 1859, there is considerable debate about "forcible resistance."

Even if we set aside the phrase, however, Thoreau and Bartleby are frequently blurred: "Thoreau says, 'I was not born to be forced. I will breathe after my own fashion.' The statement carries with it the threat of suicide, a threat which Bartleby enacts."[6] How does Thoreau's statement carry with it "the threat of suicide"? Where in "Civil Disobedience" is anything remotely like that suggested?

3. Raymond W. Short and Richard B. Sewall, *A Manual of Suggestions for Teachers Using Short Stories for Study* (New York: Henry Holt, 1956), p. 47.

4. Chris Conkling, "Misery of Christian Joy: Conscience and Freedom in 'Bartleby, The Scrivener,'" *Literature and Belief* (1981), 79–89, p. 80.

5. Frederick Busch, "Thoreau and Melville as Cellmates," *Modern Fiction Studies*, 23 (Summer, 1977), 239–42, p. 241.

6. Ibid.

Or: Bartleby's "refusal to eat in prison—now a common political act—is a political metaphor in this story."[7] Several critics point to Bartleby's political nature, saying that he goes on "a hunger strike," which seems only natural if one sees his occupation of the Lawyer's office as a "sit-in."[8]

Or: "It seems almost inevitable that Melville had Thoreau's work distinctly in mind," and we should see "something heroic" in Bartleby because his "denial has an affirmative quality, as it did when Thoreau refused to pay taxes to a government that supported slavery and war."[9] Where do we work up the assurance, since nowhere in any of Melville's published or private writing does he mention Thoreau by name, that it was "almost inevitable" that he had Thoreau "distinctly in mind"?

But Thoreau is a stalking-horse. The political readings of the story are almost always accompanied by denigrations of the Lawyer-narrator. The tragedy of Bartleby must be the Lawyer's fault, for his "final exclamation, linking Bartleby and humanity, is a way of merging the individual into the vast human tide for which he need take no responsibility." Bartleby is a victim of "the numbing world of capitalist profit and alienated labor."[10] This is familiar Marxist criticism: "The story is designed as a weapon to destroy the bourgeois reader's confidence in the value centers and habits of mind that hold his society in place."[11] We are told that "the law-

7. Ibid., p. 241.

8. Marvin Fisher, "'Bartleby,' Melville's Circumscribed Scrivener," *Southern Review*, 10 (January, 1974), 54–79, p. 64.

9. Robert E. Morseberger, "'I Prefer Not To': Melville and the Theme of Withdrawal." *University College Quarterly*, 10 (January, 1965), 24–29, p. 25.

10. Louise K. Barnett, "Bartleby as Alienated Worker," *Studies in Short Fiction*, 11 (Fall, 1974), 379–95, pp. 384–85.

11. Stephen Zelnick, "Melville's 'Bartleby': History, Ideology, and Literature," *Marxist Perspectives*, 2 (Winter, 1979–80), 74–92, p. 75.

yer's paternalism simply precludes any acknowledgement of his employees' autonomy."[12] The Lawyer gives Turkey a secondhand coat, and anyone who sees it as an act of charity should be more tough-minded, should see what it really is, a subtle way of avoiding a raise in pay. The narrator shows "intense resentment" when Turkey "tries to assert his dignity by stubbornly refusing to show gratitude for the gift." In his anonymity Bartleby himself "suggests the faceless, unknown workers of the factory."[13] (But why, one wonders, is Bartleby a member of the lumpen proletariat?—he talks and behaves like an impoverished aristocrat.) All these readings ask us to see that the subtitle is essential: "A Story of Wall Street" is "a story about class relations and their consequences."[14]

As a side consequence of the argument, modern critics play with the names of the other characters. One reader asserts that Turkey, Nippers, and Ginger Nut are slave names, like Sambo and Quimbo. We are told that the Lawyer even "advances the white man's burden argument" that Bartleby must have been sent by Providence as his "special burden on earth." In this reading Bartleby is "a slave who pays the price of insurrection" and ends "a slave" to the Lawyer's memory.[15] The names of the other scriveners "are indicative of their diminished humanity" in their employer's mind, for he has given them these "demeaning nicknames which turn them into things."[16] In the story itself, however,

12. Michael T. Gilmore, *American Romanticism and the Marketplace* (Chicago: University of Chicago Press, 1985), p. 135.

13. Ibid., p. 133.

14. Ibid., p. 132.

15. Scott Donaldson, "The Dark Truth of *The Piazza Tales*," *PMLA*, 85 (October, 1970), p. 1086.

16. The first phrase is Gilmore's, the second, Fisher's.

we are told "these may seem names, the like of which are not usually found in the Directory. In truth they were nicknames, mutually conferred upon each other by my three clerks." You could say the Lawyer is lying—if he is the capitalist swine the critics tell us he is, then he certainly would not hesitate to deceive us about the way he named his wage slaves.

How quickly, and how very far, we have come: from what might be a sly allusion to Thoreau we have full-blown political readings of the story as essentially class-conscious both in its very origin and its largest meaning—a full-scale indictment of capitalist society.

"Civil Disobedience" is, in my opinion, the greatest single essay ever written by an American; the splendor of its prose and the energy of its ideas are almost unbearable in their beauty and moral force. It is hard to exaggerate the essay's influence, for it extends around the world to Gandhi (Thoreau did see the waters of Walden Pond mixing with the sacred waters of the Ganges), and it comes home again to Martin Luther King, Jr. If Melville is truly talking about Thoreau in "Bartleby," we had better see it. Surely one of the main points of an American Renaissance course involves the conversation of the individual masterpieces. The authors all talked to each other; their lives were intimately connected. From the very beginning Thoreau was accused of picking up apples in Emerson's orchard; one cannot imagine Thoreau without understanding his long and intimate relationship with Emerson. And Robert Lowell has suggested that Emerson's single finest piece of writing was his funerary tribute to Thoreau. Similarly, *Moby-Dick* cannot be "explained" by its dedicatory note, but it would surely be perilous to ignore the capital letters on the first page:

The Silence of Bartleby

IN TOKEN
OF MY ADMIRATION FOR HIS GENIUS
THIS BOOK IS INSCRIBED
TO
NATHANIEL HAWTHORNE

Down in Brooklyn Walt Whitman sits "simmering, simmering, simmering," waiting for Emerson to bring him to a boil. When John Brown went berserk in blood and horror, Hawthorne said, "No man was ever more justly hanged," and Emerson saw Brown's execution making "the gallows more glorious than the cross." Here is the heyday of abolitionism; the Civil War lies just ahead: all these writers are talking to each other, often face to face, about the great issues of the day, about cosmic issues and little personal things. Surely the Bartleby Industry is not working overtime when it sees Melville's references in *Moby-Dick* to the American scene—to Calhoun, to Webster, to Emerson, to Polk, to the Mexican War, to slavery. "Civil Disobedience" was available to Melville from 1849 onward, in the *Aesthetic Papers*, edited by Elizabeth Peabody, Sophia Hawthorne's sister. It would in no way disfigure our sense of the fundamental way Melville's imagination works to see a refractory Thoreau lurking there somewhere in the refractory Bartleby. To deny it seems like denying that Hawthorne had Emerson on his mind when he climbed aboard "The Celestial Railroad." Melville published only two things in 1853, "Bartleby" and "Cock-A-Doodle-Do!" Almost everybody agrees that Thoreau appears in the latter, so why should we close the door on him in the former? The allusion may be slight, and may not be the point of it all, any more than Daniel Webster is Moby-Dick because they both have high foreheads, but surely there is something to it.

In my American Renaissance course I have the students

read "Benito Cereno," and I present them with two radically incompatible interpretations of it. Yvor Winters seems to have no second thoughts about how one should read the story:

When Cereno is finally rescued by Captain Delano, he is broken in spirit, and says that he can return home but to die. When Captain Delano inquires what has cast such a shadow upon him, he answers: "the negro." His reply in Spanish would have signified not only the negro, or the black man, but by metaphorical extension the basic evil in human nature. The morality of slavery is not an issue in this story; the issue is this, that through a series of acts of performance and of negligence, the fundamental evil of a group of men, evil which normally should have been kept in abeyance, was freed to act. The story is a portrait of that evil in action, as shown in the negroes, and of the effect of the action, as shown in Cereno. It is appalling in its completeness, in its subtle horror, and in its silky quiet.[17]

Is Winters right? Darrel Abel does not think so:

Babo is as much the hero of *Benito Cereno* as anyone else; the suppressed forces of life have as much inherent right to assert themselves as the rest, have as much right as the rest to thrust out of sight whatever is antagonistic to them, denies their full reality, and is to *them* the dark—that is the incomprehensible and threatening—half of the world. Aboard the *San Dominick* it was the blacks, not the Spaniards, who exhibited the full range of human vitality. Although Captain Delano had taken Babo for an "indisputable inferior" with "a limited mind," his brain was a "hive of subtlety," and he at last confronted his fate with more dignity than did Don Benito, who fainted when asked to appear in court to identify Babo. The majestic black Atufal was a figure of more personal majesty

17. Yvor Winters, *In Defense of Reason* (Denver: Allan Swallow, 1947), p. 222.

> than any of the whites, and more fit to command than his master. The American captain saw in the affection of the Negresses for their babies "pure tenderness and love." "He was gratified with their manners; like most uncivilized women, they seemed at once tender of heart and tough of constitution." It will not do to interpret the mutinous blacks of *Benito Cereno* as the representatives of evil. They represent an oppressed portion of humanity asserting its equal right to life.[18]

Winters is surely on Abel's mind—notice the line about how "it will not do" to interpret the blacks as "the representatives of evil." But can you say that Melville, in 1855, thought in any such terms as Abel's?

Scholarly articles produced in the late 1960s and 1970s demonstrate convincingly that Melville conceives Captain Delano along the lines of "the stock Yankee traveler in plantation fiction" and Don Benito in terms of "the Southern planter, the dissipated cavalier spiritually wasted by his own terrifying enslavement."[19] Scholars have shown us clear associations of Babo with Toussaint L'Ouverture. Robert Lowell adapted "Benito Cereno" to the stage as "The Old Glory," and I attended an off-Broadway performance. The curtain-raiser was Hawthorne's "My Kinsman, Major Molineux" (done wonderfully right, the actors wearing masks, the stage machinery somehow becoming the voice of the story). In Lowell's creative modulation of "Benito Cereno," the most shocking moment came when Babo shaved Don Benito: there before us was an immensely tall Don Benito

18. Darrel Abel, *American Literature* (Great Neck, N.Y.: Barron's Education Series, 1963), 2:422.

19. Eric J. Sundquist sums up the scholarship and offers his own provocative reading in "*Benito Cereno* and New World Slavery," *Reconstructing American Literary History*, ed. Sacvan Bercovitch (Cambridge: Harvard University Press, 1986), 93–122.

Cereno, with a Spanish flag spread over him as a barber's sheet, and there was Babo in a gunny-sack loin cloth, his bright razor flicking and nicking the suds on the face of the white man. The night I saw it, the sold-out auditorium was utterly hushed, except for one middle-aged black man in the front row, almost under the scene, who got possessed of uncontrollable laughter. There was silence everywhere in the theater except for that black man's high-pitched skittering giggle. I thought Babo might "break." I thought the actor, Roscoe Lee Browne, might say something, because it was an altogether impossible situation, that silence all around us pierced by the man down in the front row, convulsed, seeing a black slave brandishing a gleaming straight razor at a white master's soapy chin. After the performance, backstage, I saw the man from the front row standing at Roscoe Lee Browne's dressing room door. The man was apologizing, and suddenly Browne embraced him and said, "My man, don't apologize, you got the *point!*" The point? Whose point? Was it Melville's point back there, or is it Lowell's point now?

Haunted by the sound of that high-pitched laughter, I reread the shaving scene. Lowell had not violated its meaning, nor had he added a new one. After Babo makes a gesture as if to begin, he suddenly stops and "midway stood suspended for an instant, one hand elevating the razor, the other professionally dabbling among the bubbling suds on the Spaniard's lank neck. Not unaffected by the close sight of the gleaming steel, Don Benito nervously shuddered." Watching the scene—which has no counterpart in Melville's source, the real Amassa Delano's *Narrative of Voyages and Travels*—Delano fancies that "in the black he saw a headsman, and in the white a man at the block." Delano exclaims, "This is the flag of Spain you use here." Three times—"the steel glanced nigh the throat"—Babo says, "Now, Master." And Delano concludes, "Ah, this slavery breeds ugly passions in man." The idea of the scene and all the details in it powerfully convey what Lowell brought to the stage and what proved so difficult for the black man in the front row. I do not see how one can think of "Benito Cereno" in terms of moral allegory, literally in black and white terms, with all the traditional associations of "black" and "white." The story was published "three years after *Uncle Tom's Cabin* and not quite six before Fort Sumter."[20] How could Melville not have "the morality of slavery" on his mind?

In the prose supplement to *Battle-Pieces* Melville says, "Those of us who always abhorred slavery as an atheistical antiquity, gladly we join the exulting chorus of humanity over its downfall." In *The Piazza Tales* he puts in a note "from a private MS" at the beginning of "The Bell-Tower": "Like negroes, these powers own man sullenly; mindful of their higher master; while serving, plot revenge." If the morality of slavery is not on Melville's mind, why does he change the original date of Amassa Delano's story, 1805, to 1799, when Toussaint led the bloody uprising in Santo Domingo? Why does he change the name of the ship to the *San Dominick?* Surely Melville addressed himself to the chief social issues of his day. Earlier in his career he had written impressively about social injustice. For example, in *Redburn* we find moving passages about the slums of Liverpool and the immigrants confined like animals down in the ship's steerage. In *White Jacket* Melville's vehement protests against flogging in the U.S. Navy were instrumental in the abolition of the practice. *Moby-Dick* is full of examples in which he addresses himself to the plight of the wretched victims of capitalist

20. Sue Lonoff, "Reluctant Readers and a Controversial Classic: Teaching *Benito Cereno*," *College English*, 41 (September, 1979), 88–93, p. 91.

exploitation. Perhaps only William Faulkner belongs with him, as an American novelist who discovers in the horrors of history something to energize and occupy his deepest imaginative energy. Scholars are true to that energy when they try to find a political dimension to "Bartleby, The Scrivener." Whether we look back to *Redburn*, *White Jacket*, and *Moby-Dick*, or forward to "Benito Cereno" and *The Confidence Man*, we see that Melville's fictional worlds resonate with themes from the real one.

Mark Winsome in *The Confidence Man* is a satiric portrait of Emerson. Some critical reservations have been expressed about seeing Thoreau in Winsome's sidekick, Egbert, but he certainly looks like Thoreau with "his sharp nose and shaved chin" and his costume "modeled upon his master's." When Mark Winsome says, "I seldom care to be consistent," Melville is of course nodding at the hobgoblin of little minds, just as Emerson's ideas of "The Poet" are in Winsome's expostulation that "poetry is not a thing of ink and rhyme, but of thought and act." Egbert is Thoreau standing there "in the attitude less of an equal companion apparently than a confidential follower." Winsome says that "Egbert was the first among mankind to reduce to practice the principles of Mark Winsome"; he turns to him and says, "Now, as in a glass, you, Egbert, in your life, reflect to me the more important part of my system." Emerson and Thoreau are in *The Confidence Man*, in 1857; why couldn't they be in "Bartleby, The Scrivener" in 1853? Indeed, Emerson is already there, in Melville's rich play with "The Transcendentalist," and one or more of Thoreau's essays might provide Melville with something along those lines. Does Thoreau have to wait until he is Egbert, and Emerson is Mark Winsome, for them to walk hand in hand in Melville's imagination?

The idea that "I prefer not to" is an echo of "Civil Disobedience" can be traced back at least forty years to Egbert S. Oliver's essay "A Second Look at Bartleby."[21] Oliver starts, as many critics do, by playing with the meaning of the word "copyist." Bartleby is a "copyist," and so is Thoreau (he copies Emerson). Bartleby and Thoreau spend a lot of time looking out the window. In "Resistance to Civil Government" Thoreau says, about his overnight in jail, "I saw that if one stayed there long, his principal business would be to look out the window." In "Bartleby" the Lawyer mentions several times that Bartleby doesn't go anywhere; instead,

> for long periods he would stand looking out, at his pale window behind the screen, upon the dead brick wall.

> The next day I noticed that Bartleby did nothing but stand at his window in his dead-wall revery.

> Bartleby remained standing at his window in one of his profoundest dead-wall reveries.

What Thoreau tells us he did is what the narrator says Bartleby does: "his principal business" is "to look out the window."

And it seems at least possible to hear echoes of things Thoreau said elsewhere. From *A Week on the Concord and Merrimack Rivers*, for example: "We do not wish for Friends to feed and clothe our bodies, but to do the like office to our spirits." That may prefigure the Lawyer's anguished cry, "I might give alms to his body; but his body did not pain him; it was his soul that suffered, and his soul I could not reach." Oliver's idea is that Melville is not so much borrowing as

21. Egbert S. Oliver, "A Second Look at Bartleby," *College English*, 6 (May, 1945), 431–39.

parodying, that "Bartleby is a *reductio ad absurdum* of the convictions Thoreau expressed." Bartleby's "I would prefer not to" is a summing up, a kind of utterly negative grand finale to Thoreau's refractory insistences:

> I declined to pay.
> I can afford to refuse allegiance.
> I was not born to be forced.
> I simply wish to withdraw and stand aloof.

And these obdurate sentences, taken together, certainly begin to sound like Bartleby. We hardly have the massive moral force of Thoreau's taking on government itself, but that would be the point, in a *reductio ad absurdum.* It is like the Frank and Charlie show in *The Confidence Man.* To object to the identification of Thoreau and Bartleby because they are so different does not prove anything; Melville's whole point is to reduce Thoreau to absurdity, to push him to a ridiculous extreme, to make him funny. Melville is doing something like what he does in "Cock-A-Doodle-Do!" Bartleby does not go anywhere, by looking out the window, and Thoreau goes everywhere (as far as Germany anyway) when he looks out his jailhouse window. The difference does not prove there is no reference; the difference suggests real and substantial reference. Melville is turning Thoreau on his head, or knocking the wind out of him, or kicking his legs out from under him. Thoreau says his jailers did not understand him because they thought his chief desire was to stand on the other side of that stone wall; Oliver says, "Bartleby might well have said—or thought—the same."

Strenuous voices objected to the idea forty years ago, when Oliver first suggested it. Alfred Kazin complained that Bartleby is not Thoreau and the very idea is "intellectually vulgar."[22] There is no hint anywhere that Melville thought Thoreau's life to be "one of final negation." Kazin objected to something in Oliver's article that is quite like what I have been objecting to in the Bartleby Industry: "it turns out that the relationship is no longer 'possible' but has been proved . . . Mr. Oliver thinks it is safe to say that Bartleby is *really* Thoreau." And "surely a little less bookish source-hunting, a little more awareness of what attracts us to Melville" would be a better way to invest our energy. More recently, Hershel Parker finds Oliver's parallels unconvincing. But, he notes, Melville did visit the Hawthornes in Concord in December of 1852 "while Thoreau was apparently in residence."[23] And there is reason to believe Melville was familiar with Thoreau, because Melville knew about Horace Greeley's efforts to get Thoreau's name before the public via the New York *Herald Tribune*. We know Melville read the preface to *Mosses from an Old Manse*, in which Thoreau's name is mentioned. Parts of *A Yankee in Canada* appeared in *Putnam's* early in 1853 ("Bartleby" appears in *Putnam's* late in 1853). We know Melville borrowed *A Week on the Concord and Merrimack Rivers* from Duyckinck, in 1849 or 1850; Chapter 39 of *The Confidence Man*, that glorious debunking of friendship, is probably a satire on "Wednesday" in *A Week*. After a lengthy visit from Hawthorne, in which they spent a few days talking "ontological heroics" out in the barn, Hawthorne said he was going to write up their conversation and call it "A Week on a Work-Bench in a Barn." We don't know that Melville and Thoreau

22. Alfred Kazin, "From Ishmael in His Academic Heaven," *New Yorker*, 24 (February 12, 1949), 84–89.

23. Hershel Parker, "Melville's Satire of Emerson and Thoreau: An Evaluation of the Evidence," *American Transcendental Quarterly*, 7 (Summer, 1970), 61–67, p. 65.

ever met, but we do know that Hawthorne and Thoreau were excellent friends. And Melville might be eager to talk with his father-in-law, Lemuel Shaw, the chief justice of Massachusetts, the man who wrote the decision on the fugitive slave law, about the author of an essay on "Resistance to Civil Government" (not a famous essay—not yet—and not yet "Civil Disobedience"—but there it was in the *Aesthetic Papers* of 1849, and a copy of the book was in the library of Melville's Pittsfield neighbor, Dr. Holmes).

The identification of Bartleby and Thoreau keeps coming up, in odd ways, in other essays on other subjects. Leo Marx in his celebrated piece "Melville's Parable of the Walls" does not talk much about the specific problem of Bartleby as Thoreau, but he nevertheless says that "Bartleby represents the only real, if ultimately ineffective, threat to society; his experience gives some support to Henry Thoreau's view that one lone intransigent man can shake the foundations of our institutions."[24] Marx refers here to a passage in "Civil Disobedience" that always seems to trouble my students, the passage in which Thoreau makes his fantastic claim that "if one thousand, if one hundred, if ten men whom I could name,—if ten *honest* men only,—aye, if one HONEST man, in this State of Massachusetts, *ceasing to hold slaves*, were actually to withdraw from this copartnership, and be locked up in the county jail therefor, it would be the abolition of slavery in America." Students often ask something like, "Well what if a fascist decides he doesn't like a law? Thoreau thinks he was right, and maybe he was, but how does society protect itself against fanatics? Just because you believe in something doesn't give you the right to break the law!" I constantly hear versions of that argument, and Thoreau's

24. Leo Marx, "Melville's Parable of the Walls," *Sewanee*, 61 (1953), 602–27, p. 621.

answer is right there in black and white. Somehow students don't seem to get it until you point out that you have to go to *jail*, it's *Civil* Disobedience; Martin Luther King writes his "Letter from a Birmingham *Jail*." But what Leo Marx is pointing to is that in "Bartleby" just one man prefers not to—and the whole office stops functioning, nothing can go on as before, Bartleby has mucked up the system. Are we to believe, as Marx suggests, that this "gives some support to Henry Thoreau's view"? Is "Bartleby" to be understood as Melville's profound understanding—or wry demonstration—of what Thoreau was saying? Does "Bartleby" show how a single dissenter can bring a social economy to a grinding halt? Look at Bartleby's effect on the narrator—the eminently *safe* man's snug life erupts in utter turmoil. He cannot get anything accomplished because one man says no.

What has always struck me, in this regard, are those walls. In "Civil Disobedience" Thoreau writes an extraordinary paragraph in which he mentions the walls four times:

> I stood considering the walls of solid stone, two or three feet thick

> if there was a wall of stone between me and my townsmen, there was a still more difficult one to climb through

> the walls seemed a great waste of stone and mortar

> they thought that my chief desire was to stand the other side of that stone wall

At the end of "Bartleby" the Lawyer stares at the walls and speaks forcefully about "the surrounding walls, of amazing thickness"; he tells us that "the Egyptian character of the masonry weighed upon me with its gloom." He says Bartleby has gone off to dine "with kings and counselors"—far from this jail. Thoreau, too, escapes from his local jail and goes off to a world elsewhere: "Concord was turned into a Rhine stream, and visions of knights and castles passed before me. They were the voices of old burghers that I heard in the streets." Thoreau says it was "a wholly new and rare experience." In both texts, the walls have yielded to imaginative transport. Could Melville have borrowed from Thoreau in the way he borrowed from Emerson?

We may have to reject, ultimately, a question we must ask, at least provisionally: Why hasn't anybody been able to find evidence that any contemporary reader saw Thoreau in Bartleby? Why did we have to wait a century before critics began to debate it? In the modern scholarship it is simply assumed that "passive resistance" is "Civil Disobedience"—indeed, as we have seen, several critics automatically attribute the phrase to Thoreau himself. Others insist that "I prefer not to" is an echo of Melville's letter to Hawthorne acknowledging the gift of *The House of the Seven Gables:* "There is the grand truth about Nathaniel Hawthorne. He says NO! in thunder; but the Devil himself cannot make him say *yes.*" One reader says the phrases have "the same effect" and that Bartleby's "soft-spoken refusal to join the ordinary course of life carries a strength of conviction equal to Hawthorne's emphatic 'No!'"[25] But it is not at all "the same effect." How do you say "I prefer not to" "in thunder"? "I prefer not to" begins to turn up in the speech of the other characters in an insidious way, hardly in thunder. And when Melville does actually satirize Thoreau, as Egbert in *The Confidence Man,* he gives him his big nose and shaved chin and style of dress. In none of Thoreau's self-portraits, or portraits other men drew of him, does he look or talk like

25. R. Bruce Bickley, Jr., *The Method of Melville's Shorter Tales* (Durham, N.C.: Duke University Press, 1979), p. 34.

Bartleby. Thoreau was not pale or mild or pallid or gentle or meek; he was active, vigorous, and bold. Robert Lowell has correctly identified the most striking quality of *Walden*: "all is flexibility and fire. The great sinews of syntax move without toil or ornament, page after page lover-eyed, intimate, and flashing."[26] Nothing could be farther from Bartleby.

But something else, something that may be finally more important, is troubling about the attempt to see Thoreau in Bartleby. In her essay "Bartleby and Manhattan," Elizabeth Hardwick catches herself when she writes of Bartleby's "retort."[27] No, she says, "retort" is a word that "will not do, representing as it does too great a degree of active mutuality for Bartleby." Better to say "*reply*, perhaps." Hardwick notes that "the cadaverous and yet blazing center of all our attention speaks only thirty-seven short lines," over one-third of which are variations on "I prefer not to." How do we take those utterances? We ask ourselves, "What is Bartleby thinking about when he is alone?" Immediately Hardwick answers that "one would be foolhardy to give him thoughts." Why? Because "they would dishonor him."

There we have it—in that stinging verb, *dishonor*. Hardwick asks what we would think of him if Bartleby said, "I don't want to" or "I don't feel like it." No, that would be "unthinkable, a vulgarization, adding truculence, idleness, foolishness, adding indeed 'character' and altering a sublimity of definition."[28] You cannot think of Bartleby as anybody else; to do so violates Melville's "sublimity of definition." The association of Thoreau with Bartleby politicizes Melville's story and fudges the profound emotional experience of realizing Bartleby as Bartleby.

26. Robert Lowell, *Collected Prose* (New York: Farrar Straus Giroux, 1987), p. 192.

27. Elizabeth Hardwick, "Bartleby and Manhattan," *New York Review of Books*, July 16, 1981, 27–31, p. 27.

28. Ibid., p. 28.

"A Passive Resistance"

In one of the operas made out of "Bartleby," Jay Leyda provides the words for an aria:

> What do these walls shut out?
> What do these bricks shut in?
> Behind that wall, behind every wall,
> Is another—and another—and yet another wall.
> Between the dirty bricks,
> Below every beam,
> People live—or think they live,
> And watch each other die.
> Through the walls of brick and walls of flesh,
> What man believes his fellow man?

In "Bartleby: Genesis of an Opera," Walter Aschaffenburg says, "No doubt, people will argue that putting such words into Bartleby's mouth is to alter his character considerably."[29] No, to put such words into Bartleby's mouth is not to alter him considerably—it is to change him utterly. It is, as Hardwick says, to dishonor him. The Lawyer advances an explanation for Bartleby in his concluding paragraph about the Dead Letter Office. I think we should see what the Lawyer does as a kind of helpless reaching, what a man baffled and hurt would do. Somewhere there has to be a meaning to Bartleby.

But there isn't. How long has Bartleby been sick? Is there a primal trauma? A recent crippling blow? Where does the man's trouble begin? Nowhere. Nowhere that one can tell. Bartleby is intractable. If he means anything other than the riddle of himself, he is not who he is. Bartleby is Thoreau? No, the whole point of Bartleby, the maddening and precious thing about him, is that he is a lost cause. He is inconsolable.

29. Both Leyda and Aschaffenburg are quoted in *Melville Annual 1965, A Symposium: "Bartleby the Scrivener,"* ed. Howard P. Vincent (Kent, Ohio: Kent State University Press, 1966), p. 37.

CHAPTER 4

"Hawthorne: A Problem"

(April 16? 1851)

My Dear Hawthorne—

. . . "The House of the Seven Gables: A Romance. By Nathaniel Hawthorne. One vol, 16 mos, pp. 344." The contents of this book do not belie its rich, clustering, romantic title. With great enjoyment we spent almost an hour in each separate gable. This book is like a fine old chamber, abundantly, but still judiciously, furnished with precisely that sort of furniture best fitted to furnish it. There are rich hangings, wherein are braided scenes from tragedies! There is old china with rare devices, set out on the carved buffet; there are long and indolent lounges to throw yourself upon; there is an admirable sideboard, plentifully stored with good viands; there is a smell as of old wine in the pantry; and finally, in one corner, there is a dark little black-letter volume in golden clasps, entitled "Hawthorne: A Problem."

R. Bruce Bickley, Jr., proposes that "Hawthorne himself sat for the portrait of Bartleby."[1] We are told that Hawthorne's "Fire Worship" leads to Melville's "I and My Chimney," Hawthorne's "Sights from a Steeple" leads to Melville's "The Two Temples," and Bartleby is prefigured in Hawthorne's nay-saying characters Young Goodman Brown and Parson Hooper. Bickley says the following lines about Vine, the Hawthorne figure in Melville's

1. R. Bruce Bickley, Jr., "The Minor Fiction of Hawthorne and Melville," *American Transcendental Quarterly*, 14 (1972), 149–52, p. 149.

long poem *Clarel*, suggest Bartleby. At the end, facing the wall of the Tombs, his eyes open, is Vine:

> But who is he uncovered seen,
> Profound in shadow of the tomb
> Reclined, with meditative mien
> Intent upon the tracery?
>
> (I. xxviii. ll. 37–40)

This association extends what several critics see in that telling detail at the end of "Bartleby," that he lost his job because "he had been suddenly removed by a change in the administration." This, say the critics, is Melville's knowing reference to Hawthorne's essay "The Custom-House," in which Hawthorne tells us how he lost his surveyor's job due to a change in the administration.

Walter Evans argues that Nathaniel Hawthorne is a character in the story—not Bartleby, but the Lawyer. Melville is "largely 'copying' the Lawyer's personality from Hawthorne's."[2] At the time Melville wrote "Bartleby" he was experiencing "an intense psychic identification with Hawthorne" (he had dedicated his masterpiece to him), and when Hawthorne moved from the Berkshires to West Newton, "Melville, like Bartleby, then progressively and passively withdrew." Life and Art seem to be much the same: "After being abandoned, Bartleby remains where he is, as did Melville." Details in the story make poignant new sense in this light: Hawthorne's efforts to help Melville get a consulship at Hawaii and Antwerp are the basis for the Lawyer's encouraging Bartleby to get another job that doesn't involve

2. Walter Evans, "Hawthorne and 'Bartleby, The Scrivener,'" *American Transcendental Quarterly*, no. 57 (1985), 45–58, p. 51.

writing. The Lawyer's relationship to Astor is based on Hawthorne's relationship to Franklin Pierce. Just as Melville modeled some of his work on Hawthorne's, so "the scrivener copies what the lawyer originally writes." When Melville tells the story from Hawthorne's point of view, he is trying to understand why Hawthorne rejected him. He expected Hawthorne to read it and was "confronting Hawthorne with the terrible need he had ignored": "Melville devotes immense psychological energy to analyzing and understanding reactions and motivations of a man whom he deeply loved and yet could hardly help bitterly resenting."[3] "Bartleby" is "a desolate response to the rejection" Melville felt when Hawthorne abandoned him.

Now we are in trouble. How can Nathaniel Hawthorne be both Bartleby and the Lawyer? Various details in the arguments are unconvincing, but the difficulty lies not with particular points. There is something drastically wrong with the idea itself. The friendship between Nathaniel Hawthorne and Herman Melville was perhaps the most intense in our literature, between two great writers—at least for a while, at least on Melville's part. But it would be misguided, I think, to read that friendship into the story so that Hawthorne is actually embodied there, allegorically represented, rushing around in the person of the Lawyer or standing still in the figure of Bartleby.

Hawthorne's work, not Hawthorne the man, might appear in "Bartleby." Melville could have used Hawthorne's scenes or characters or actual lines of prose. Melville did so with Emerson, a man he scarcely knew, and he would more likely do so with a man he loved, a man whose work had

3. Ibid., p. 55.

filled him with a "shock of recognition." Leo B. Levy has proposed that this is what happened. He asserts that "Bartleby" "came directly out of" and "specifically as a response to" Hawthorne's "Old Apple Dealer."[4]

In Melville's "Hawthorne and His Mosses," the discussion of "The Old Apple Dealer" is preceded by brief remarks about the orchard of the Old Manse and the humorous sketches "Buds and Bird-Voices" and "Fire-Worship." They have their charm, Melville says, but that is the problem. Their charm is why readers have been misguided about Hawthorne and failed to hear his essential voice. Readers think him "a pleasant writer, with a pleasant style—a sequestered, harmless man, from whom any deep and weighty thing would hardly be anticipated:—a man who means no meanings." After his polite nod at the "richly relishable good humor," Melville turns to the other Hawthorne, the Hawthorne who "has still other apples," the Hawthorne Melville wants to talk about, the author of "the sketch of 'The Old Apple Dealer.'" In that portrait we find "the subtlest spirit of sadness"; Melville quotes from it to show that "such touches as are in this piece can not proceed from any common heart." Melville usually reads Hawthorne's works to find clues about the man who wrote them, and so he does here: Melville says "The Old Apple Dealer" argues

> such a depth of tenderness, such a boundless sympathy with all forms of being, such an omnipresent love, that we must needs say, that this Hawthorne is almost alone in his generation,—at least in the artistic manifestation of these things. Still more. Such touches as these,—and many, very many similar ones, all through his chapters—furnish clews, whereby we enter a little way into the intricate, profound heart where they originated.

4. Leo B. Levy, "Hawthorne and the Idea of 'Bartleby,'" *Emerson Society Quarterly*, 47 (1967), 66–69, p. 66.

Melville goes on directly to praise Hawthorne's "great, deep intellect, which drops down into the universe like a plummet." Melville finds in these tales "that blackness in Hawthorne, of which I have spoken, that so fixes and fascinates me." It is the essential Hawthorne, a man who makes "those short, quick probings at the very axis of reality": "This Hawthorne has dropped germinous seeds into my soul. He expands and deepens down, the more I contemplate him; and further, and further, shoots his strong New-England roots into the hot soil of my Southern soul." Melville wrote this essay almost exactly three years before he wrote "Bartleby." It would seem entirely natural that when he sat down to compose his first short story he would look back to Hawthorne's stories and his review of them. The first "serious" short story he had found to praise was "The Old Apple Dealer."

Hawthorne says that "the lover of the moral picturesque . . . may sometimes find what he seeks in a character which is nevertheless of too negative a description to be seized upon and represented to the imaginative vision by word painting." This seems suggestive, for Melville's Lawyer describes the view from his office as "deficient in what landscape painters call 'life.'" Hawthorne's slightly scornful phrase "the lover of the moral picturesque" may foreshadow the Lawyer's phrase about how "good-natured gentlemen might smile, and sentimental souls might weep." Hawthorne says he has "studied the old apple dealer until he has become a naturalized citizen of my inner world," and "it is a strange witchcraft whereby this faded and featureless old apple dealer has gained a settlement in my memory." He certainly looks like Bartleby—"this almost hueless object"—"poor, neglected, friendless, unappreciated, and with little that demands appreciation," this man who offers "gingerbread and apples" for sale. (And with those two telling details, exactly the same, how can we not think of the office on Wall Street?)

Hawthorne tells us that the "frost-bitten aspect" of the old apple dealer "is a moral frost which no physical warmth or comfortableness could counteract." We are reminded of the Lawyer's cry that he could comfort Bartleby's physical wants, but "his soul I could not reach." In Hawthorne's description, the old apple dealer is very much like Bartleby:

> It is a patient, long-suffering, quiet, hopeless, shivering aspect. He is not desperate,—that, though its etymology implies no more, would be too positive an expression,—but merely devoid of hope.

> He can never suffer the extreme of misery, because the tone of his whole being is too much subdued for him to feel any thing acutely.

He "speaks to none," for "activity in business would require an energy that never could have been a characteristic of his almost passive disposition even in youth." He resumes "the lifelong, frozen patience in which consists his strength." Bartleby is here. The old apple dealer "never speaks an unnecessary word"; "he makes the briefest possible response to all general remarks, and shrinks quietly into himself again." That is Bartleby. His sigh, "so faint as to be hardly perceptible, and not expressive of any definite emotion, is the accompaniment and conclusion of all his actions. It is the symbol of the chilliness and torpid melancholy of his old age." That is not Bartleby. Hawthorne's apple dealer is a portrait of old age, and "you pity him without a scruple." There is no refractory quality to him, none of Bartleby's inscrutable dignity. Here is pity, unreserved and unchecked, quite unlike the Lawyer's contradictory feelings. The apple dealer is just an old man—except—"his life has all been of a piece." Hawthorne's speaker tries to fill in the blanks, perhaps prefiguring the Lawyer's attempts to do so with Bartleby: of the old apple dealer we may conclude that "he was perhaps a mechanic, who never came to be a master in his craft, or a petty tradesman, rubbing onward between passably to do and poverty." But that is no Dead Letter Office. Hawthorne is musing about something sad; he is not the Lawyer rushing in with a frantic need to explain. Hawthorne's conclusion has a platitudinous and affirmative quality: "Could I read but a tithe of what is written there, it would be a volume of deeper and more comprehensive import than all that the wisest mortals have given to the world; for the soundless depths of the human soul and of eternity have an opening through your breast." The sigh and the shiver "shall flit upward" and be at peace. There is no mystery here, as there is with Bartleby. The apple dealer is a sweet old man. Hawthorne ends, "And now farewell, old friend!"—a pretty standard benediction, not the Lawyer's anguished cry.

But maybe Hawthorne's sudden imaginative realization "I have him now" prefigures the Lawyer's fit of insight, "At last I see it, I feel it." There is a lot here that does work, not only the apple and gingerbread, but also the very similar descriptions of an isolated, dignified, unreachable man. We know Melville picked out this story to start talking about what thrilled him when he read *Mosses from an Old Manse* in the summer of 1850. We know that in the summer of 1853 Melville was trying his hand at his first short story. And we know Hawthorne had just moved away and that Melville was desperately trying to reach him, writing ferverish letters, debating with him about which one of them could do the better job with the material for a short story.

Melville loved Hawthorne, loved him deeply. Surely that love speaks in the pages of "Bartleby." The Lawyer comes out of the "eminently *safe*" and cloistered life he has led; as the story goes on, he feels a great love for the solitary scrivener whom the seas of life have washed up at his door. But what good does love do? love cannot reach, cannot save. Death is stronger than love. It is nobody's fault. When Hawthorne died, Melville began his anguished "Monody":

> To have known him, to have loved him
> After loneness long;
> And then to be estranged in life,
> And neither in the wrong—

Several years later, in *Clarel*, Melville looked back to Hawthorne, and his portrait is all delicacy:

> Pure as the rain
> Which diamondeth with lucid grain
> The white swan in the April hours . . .

Can it be altogether wrong to read backward into "Bartleby" such exquisite expressions of love? Is it wrong to read the passionate sentences of "Hawthorne and His Mosses" forward into "Bartleby"? Surely, too, we neglect at our peril the lavish rambunctiousness of Herman's feelings for Nathaniel. In a P.S. to his November 17, 1851, letter, Melville said:

> I should have a paper-mill established at one end of the house, and so have an endless riband of foolscap rolling in upon my desk; and upon that endless riband I should write a thousand—a million—billion thoughts, all under the form of a letter to you. The divine magnet is on you, and the magnet responds. Which is the biggest? A foolish question—they are *One*.

All through these letters there is a sense of uncontrollable and overwhelming love (especially the two letters in June,

1851). We do not do untoward violence in saying these are "love letters." And we do not neglect Hawthorne to say those letters have as much to do with the composition of *Moby-Dick* as they do with the man to whom they are addressed. No, the conventional story is correct: *Moby-Dick* and Hawthorne are all mixed up together in Melville's mind, and when he speaks of one, he speaks of the other. When Melville receives Hawthorne's letter about *Moby-Dick* he cries out: "Whence come you, Hawthorne? By what right do you drink from my flagon of life? And when I put it to my lips—lo, they are yours and not mine. I feel that the Godhead is broken up like the bread at the Supper, and that we are the pieces." This is the letter in which Herman Melville says to Nathaniel Hawthorne, "Knowing you persuades me more than the Bible of our Immortality." Hawthorne is intensely there in Melville's imagination, energizing it with enormous power. Leon Howard says that "of all Melville's recorded acquaintances, Hawthorne seems to have come nearest satisfying, during a brief period of creative excitement and need, that desire for companionship" which was crucial.[5] Melville writes to Hawthorne that "in my proud, humble way—a shepherd king,—I was lord of a little vale in solitary Crimea; but you have now given me the crown of India," and at that moment "your heart beat in my ribs and mine in yours, and both in God's."

But these joyous ejaculations stop; they are missing even in 1852. For whatever the reason, there is more anxiousness than ecstasy in the letters now. Much of it may have to do with the drastic change in Melville's own situation, rather than in his relationship with Hawthorne—or, one should say, Melville's relationship with anyone could hardly fail to

5. Leon Howard, *Herman Melville: A Biography* (Berkeley: University of California Press, 1951), p. 300.

be changed utterly by the heroic composition of *Moby-Dick* and the intense labors of writing *Pierre* at white heat before giving himself time to recover. And then, the world rejected both.

A few years later, when they meet in Liverpool, Hawthorne notes that Melville "certainly is much overshadowed since I saw him last." Or, perhaps he looks "much as he used to do, a little paler, and perhaps a little sadder"; for here he is, "in a rough outside coat, and with his characteristic gravity and reserve of manner." Hawthorne wonders if the great change in Melville may be only that "he has been affected with neuralgic complaints in his head and limbs, and no doubt has suffered from too constant literary occupation, pursued without much success, latterly." And "his writings, for a long while past, have indicated a morbid state of mind." His trip to the Holy Land may do him good; he needs to "take an airing through the world, after so many years of toilsome pen-labor." (Hawthorne adds a wry little note: "He is a person of very gentlemanly instincts in every respect, save that he is a little heterodox in the matter of clean linen.") For all the critics have said about the tragic betrayal or rupture or abandonment or whatever we choose to call it, there is Hawthorne's generous coda: "He can neither believe, nor be comfortable in his unbelief; and he is too honest and courageous not to try to do one or the other. If he were a religious man, he would be one of the most truly religious and reverential; he has a very high and noble nature, and better worth immortality than most of us."[6]

At the end of his life, Melville was still remembering Hawthorne: Billy Budd "has as much of masculine beauty as one can expect anywhere to see; nevertheless, like the beauti-

6. *The English Notebooks of Nathaniel Hawthorne*, ed. Randall Stewart (New York: Modern Language Association of America, 1941), pp. 432–33.

ful woman in one of Hawthorne's minor tales, there was just one thing amiss in him. No visible blemish, indeed, as with the lady; no, but an occasional liability to a vocal defect." Such a reference may catch us by surprise, as we are engrossed with the *Rights of Man*, the perfidy of Claggart, the tragic dilemma of Captain Vere. But that allusion to "The Birthmark" can send us back forty years to that famous picnic in Stockbridge, Massachusetts, when Melville met Hawthorne for the first time. The celebrated young author of *Typee*, just turned thirty-one, ran out on an overhanging rock, playing sailor; that night in the twilight the famous, finally famous, author of *The Scarlet Letter*, forty-six, followed the revelers through the dusk, calling out to them that certain destruction was inevitable to their whole party.

Melville complained to Hawthorne that it was awful to be known as a man who had lived among cannibals, awful to be doomed to go down to posterity that way. He felt his unique experience, and his fame for it, had denied him the latitude to explore his profounder imaginings. He did not enjoy being backed into a corner or put on a shelf where the public wanted him to duplicate his early adventure stories. Melville's urgent desire not to be a copyist is, for some critics, the real meaning of a story about a pale scrivener in a law office. Michael T. Gilmore reads the ending of "Bartleby" as Melville's way of saying that

> to write fiction subversive of the current order of things is to resign oneself to the composition of texts without readers; this, surely, is one more meaning of the phrase "dead letters." . . . "I want nothing to say to you" Bartleby declares when the lawyer visits him in prison. In these words, practically the last spoken by the scrivener, it is indeed possible to sense Melville's withdrawal from fiction.

In "Bartleby" Melville "disavows the possibility of a personal author-audience relation, taking the alienation of the working class as a figure for his own estrangement from the public."[7]

Our interest here is the relationship between Hawthorne and Melville, and it may clarify the problem if we look at how Gilmore articulates his idea with regard to Hawthorne. The characters in *The Scarlet Letter* are seen as allegorical embodiments of the author's anxiety about the way his audience reads what he writes:

> The difference in status and behavior of Hawthorne's principal characters dramatizes the conflict in his mind between two radically opposed conceptions of the artist's role and relation to the public. On the one side is the version of the artist represented by Hester, a scorned outcast who makes no compromises with her audience and is indifferent to its approval. If she cannot speak the truth in the marketplace, she will not speak there at all.[8]

But, I wonder, what writer is not mad about the "marketplace," about reaching a readership? That seems to me more like an occupational hazard than a social comment. Hester Prynne is not worried about all the trash that sells; she is not what Gilmore says she is, "the first full-length representation in American literature of the alienated modern artist." Poor Hester has enough problems on her hands in seventeenth-century Boston. Gilmore goes on to assert that "Dimmesdale, who embodies the other side of Hawthorne's thinking, is a type of the artist for whom fame and popularity are everything." Dimmesdale is a nineteenth-century novelist, too, and at the end of the book he "ceases

7. Michael T. Gilmore, *American Romanticism and the Marketplace* (Chicago: University of Chicago Press, 1985), p. 145.

8. Ibid., p. 76.

his false life of pandering to the popular taste."[9] If we forget the time in which the book is set and concentrate instead on the time in which it was written, we see that Dimmesdale is tired of being Fanny Fern. *Very* tired, for "the writer 'dies.'"

This 1980s argument strikes me as something akin to what the "Symbol" critics argued in the 1950s. It may not ring with the universal resonance of the fifties (we have tightened our belts for the eighties, and we are talking about the writer's "marketplace"), but in both schools of thought literature seems to be not about the world; rather, literature *is* the world, and literary characters are merely the reflections of their creators' dilemmas. When writers put words down on paper, the words are finally about putting words down on paper. Such a notion parochializes literature and limits rather severely its claims on our attention.

But the very best Melville scholars see "Bartleby, The Scrivener" as an artist fable. Richard Chase and Newton Arvin are among the most insistent; both propose that the story can be understood best as a story about writing.

Chase starts out with a prudent disclaimer: "Bartleby" goes with the works around it, and

> the writings of this period unmistakably indicate Melville's nervous instability and his deep unhappiness. . . . Still, it is misleading to assume that after 1852 Melville was plunged into impotent despair, blind cynicism, and "morbidity." It has too often, and too easily been assumed that since Melville himself was poor, unhappy, and unhealthy after 1852, and especially during the 1853–1856 period, everything he wrote was injured by excessive introspection and pessimissm.[10]

9. Ibid., pp. 94–95.
10. Richard Chase, *Herman Melville: A Critical Study* (New York: Macmillan, 1949), pp. 142–43.

The work Melville produced during these years "gives us the impression of a man carefully probing new areas of experience and seeking out new styles." This is usually forgotten by those who see Melville suddenly in fatal decline. Melville was still a young man in 1853; he had had two terrible defeats, but "Bartleby" received unanimous praise, and *The Piazza Tales* was hailed as his return to imaginative power. Chase is correct to remind us that Melville was still very much alive.

But then Chase suggests that

> on the internal evidence of the story, there seems no doubt that Melville was consciously writing a parable of the artist. . . . Bartleby is a scrivener—that is, a writer. . . . The other scriveners, Turkey and Nippers, represent what we might now call "middle-brow" culture. They have sold out to the commercial interests and suffer from the occupational diseases of the compromised artist in a commercial society—neurosis, alcoholism, and ulcers. Their depressions and manias are equally unproductive of first-rate work, and they maintain a grudging and suspicious attitude toward Bartleby, their acknowledged superior as a scrivener—the attitude of the uneasy middle-brow toward the genuine artist.[11]

Note that we cannot take these words literally. Chase's paragraph depends on figures of speech, all of which, if you examine them closely, at least subtly and often largely violate what actually goes on in the story. The other scriveners do not think Bartleby is a "genuine artist" or "superior" to them in anything but his damned attitude; they're mad at him because he won't pull his share of the load. They have not "sold out"—they are desperately trying to make a living.

But we should not altogether cast out what may be only overemphasis. And Newton Arvin reads it this way, too. He says "Bartleby" is "doubtless a parable of the frustrated rela-

11. Ibid., p. 147.

tions between the man of letters and the man of affairs, between the artist's world and the world of practice. Bartleby has already learned that communication between writer and man is mostly impossible." He is "a thwarted writer." Arvin, like Chase, like so many critics since, sees "Bartleby" as "the tale in which Melville announced to those who could understand him that he would no longer willingly be misemployed."[12] But who are "those who could understand him?" What, where, and from whom has Bartleby "already learned" anything? Why is Bartleby a "thwarted writer"? A scrivener is not a writer. A scrivener is an amanuensis, one employed to write from dictation, a secretary, a nineteenth-century xerox machine. He does not write novels and short stories. He copies manuscripts—in this case, legal documents. Melville's whole point, Melville's explicit point, is that there is nothing creative about the job. Interpretations of the story as an artist fable all depend on making metaphors out of "copy" and "Dead Letter" and "recondite documents." To see the story as Melville's artistic autobiography is literally to fool with words. We would have to blur them slightly to begin at all; and blur them altogether to see the story as Melville's verdict on his situation in 1853 (and bring in the long silence of his later years, and read that backwards into it). Maybe that is something we should do—but not automatically. Neither the Lawyer nor Bartleby is an actual writer like Hawthorne or Melville, let alone Irving or Dickens or Poe.

In his splendid book on William Faulkner, Irving Howe objects to the knee-jerk way so many critics do this:

> The contemporary eagerness to interpret works of literature as symbolic patterns is often due to a fear or distaste of direct experi-

12. Newton Arvin, *Herman Melville* (New York: Viking, 1950), pp. 211, 242.

> ence—sometimes, of direct literary experience. It is supposed that a symbol is always deeper or more profound than the subject or condition it symbolizes. . . . This mode of interpretation supports the assumption that truth or reality is always "behind" what we see and sense. . . . This view reflects a hesitation before the rough surface of experience, a wish, perhaps, to relegate it to metaphysical category.
>
> An important critical issue is at stake here: that the critic should be loyal to the surface of the text, persist in treating it in its own terms as much as he possibly can, and "convert" to other terms only when and if there is no alternative.[13]

In so many modern readings of "Bartleby" the conversion to other terms is immediate. It is almost automatic. The story becomes an elaborate set of signals: Melville and Hawthorne are here, allegorically, and the story is about the perils of authorship.

Chase's and Arvin's books involve lengthy investigations of the way Melville's mind worked. The readings of "Bartleby" are not meant to stand by themselves; they are parts of sustained arguments, for "Bartleby" is a special example of a general idea. Neither critic makes the Hawthorne connection; both confine themselves to Melville as the significant "writer." Even so, Chase and Arvin use "Bartleby" in a way that curiously contradicts the point of their large discussions. Where is the expansive quality of Melville's mind, the scrupulously inquiring and mythic quality of it? All sorts of things may be said about Captain Ahab, but we must not forget that he is the captain of a whaling vessel. Why isn't the narrator of "Bartleby" a lawyer?

He is. And he is not concerned with plot or character

13. Irving Howe, *William Faulkner: A Critical Study* (New York: Random House, 1952), pp. 173, 255.

development; he is concerned with Chancery and precedent and doctrines of assumption. His occupation is clear in every line he speaks. Melville takes extraordinary pains to make his narrator a "real" lawyer, a convincing lawyer, a man who thinks seriously about his profession and believably practices his trade. We are in no danger of forgetting Hawthorne if we insist that Melville had other profound relationships. Melville dedicates *Moby-Dick* to a writer, but he dedicated *Typee* to a lawyer, Lemuel Shaw, his future father-in-law, the chief justice of Massachusetts. There are lawyers everywhere in Melville's families, all three families—Melville, Gansevoort, and Shaw. Melville's relationship with them was intense, especially with his brothers Allan and Gansevoort, and with his father-in-law. Melville writes about several big dinners, both in America and England, with lawyers. Everybody is dealing with lawyers in the attempt to rescue him from his ill health and send him to Honolulu or Antwerp. He refers to law and lawyers throughout his work. There are abundant legal citations and fantasies of lawyers in *Mardi*, the depositions in "Benito Cereno," the tragic questions of local military law and Ultimate Law in "Billy Budd." There are lawyers in *Pierre* with "full purses and empty heads." And there is "the Advocate" in *Moby-Dick*—and those "Fast-Fish" and "Loose-Fish"—"These pleadings, and the counter pleadings, being duly heard, the very learned judge in set terms decided, to wit. . . ." It is a crazy long essay on "the fundamentals of all human jurisprudence." In "Heads or Tails," there is that lovely verdict, "And thus there seems a reason in all things, even in law." Reference, parody, intellectual jokes, and incidental asides, deep probings of the massive role of law from small-claims court to national treaties—these are real, and we do not have to pun with them.

I would not for the world dismiss Nathaniel Hawthorne from "Bartleby, The Scrivener"; his spirit is profoundly there. Just before he wrote "Bartleby," Melville wrote to Hawthorne about "Agatha," a long-suffering woman who waited years for her husband to return to her, not knowing she had already lost him. This could be a wonderful Hawthorne story. Melville thinks so, and writes with such enthusiasm that he fears to "make you smile at my strange impertinent officiousness." But that is exactly what it is, and he cannot stop it. You, Hawthorne, must write this story, and I, Melville, will supervise the labors: "the father of Agatha must be an old widower," you "must introduce" the mail post, "Agatha should be active during the wreck," Robinson "should be ministered to."[14] Melville is full of ways to write a story of abandonment.

For all the echolalia from "The Old Apple Dealer," I suspect that another Hawthorne story had a profounder effect on "Bartleby." Melville himself mentions it: "I am reminded of your *London Husband*." That has to be "Wakefield," Hawthorne's story of how a man "under pretence of going on a journey, took lodgings in the next street to his own house, and there, unheard of by his wife or friends, and without the shadow of a reason for such self-banishment, dwelt upwards of twenty years." Melville would naturally think of Hawthorne's "*London Husband*" when he was writing to Hawthorne that Agatha's husband would perhaps have a hard time when he tried "to settle upon the exact day when he could say to himself, '*Now* I have deserted my wife.'" Wakefield, with his cunning smile, is more like Bartleby than is the pathetic old apple dealer. Wakefield's ghastly destiny is to be the "Outcast of the Universe." The

14. *The Letters of Herman Melville*, ed. Merrell R. Davis and William H. Gilman (New Haven: Yale University Press, 1960), pp. 155–58.

old apple dealer is easy to understand; Wakefield, like Bartleby, is impenetrable.

But I do not want to exchange one story for another. Hawthorne's influence on Melville cannot be understood by reference to any specific work. When the Lawyer visits Bartleby in the Tombs, he looks at the walls and sees "the Egyptian character of the masonry"; he notices, too, the "grass-seed dropped by birds" that has sprung up in the yard. Leo Marx reminds us that when Melville wrote to Hawthorne, in June of 1851, he spoke of his own soul as a "seed residing in the Egyptian Pyramids."[15] Of course, both Hawthorne and Melville were writers; of course, Melville's story has its origin in his creative predicament in 1853.

But one of our first critical jobs is to reckon with a writer's transmutative power. "A Story of Wall Street" is not an elaborate code for the modern critical mind; we should not have to crack the code to read the "real" story underneath, "A Story of Pittsfield." We shrink from our job of understanding Melville's imaginative energy when we turn his work of fiction into an autobiographical essay. Hawthorne did not take up the patient Griselda material that Melville presented to him with all that "strange impertinent officiousness"; it was not in thunder, but Hawthorne clearly said no. Stung, Melville turned from Agatha to Bartleby. Or, one should say, Melville nursed his wounds, took his time, recovered himself, and wrote his own story.

Earlier I quoted John Haag, the actor who played Bartleby; Haag complains eloquently that readers of Bartleby

15. Leo Marx, "Melville's Parable of the Walls," *Sewanee*, 61 (1953), 602–27, p. 623. Marx, too, concludes that "there are excellent reasons for reading 'Bartleby' as a parable having to do with Melville's own fate as a writer," and "there can be little doubt about the connection between Bartleby's dilemma and Melville's own" (p. 603). Marx suggests that "I prefer not to" corresponds to "Yet . . . write the *other* way I cannot" (p. 612).

"too often pursue his 'meaning' rather than recognize the intensity of his suffering."[16] This seems to me true both of the attempt to politicize the story by turning Bartleby into Thoreau and of the effort to see it as a writer fable by turning Bartleby into Hawthorne or Melville himself. The strategy is inherently evasive. It tells us what we have been trained to look for in our reading and what is considered important to say about it. This is professional reading rather than reading; gradually the text ceases to exist as an end in itself and becomes an occasion for us to express our elaborate critical and scholarly ingenuity. Such efforts to enrich the story may actually impoverish it, diverting us from the sense of wonder and pain that it provides. As Elizabeth Hardwick said, to read Bartleby as someone other than himself "dishonors" him. And it does him great violence—it takes his silence away from him.

16. Quoted by William P. Sullivan, "Bartleby and Infantile Autism: A Naturalistic Explanation," *Bulletin of the West Virginia Association of College English Teachers*, 3, no. 2 (Fall, 1976), 43–60, p. 56.

CHAPTER 5

The Reliable Narrator

> Somehow, of late, I had got into the way of involuntarily using this word "prefer" upon all sorts of not exactly suitable occasions. And I trembled to think that my contact with the scrivener had already and seriously affected me in a mental way. And what further and deeper aberration might it not yet produce?

If I had to isolate one reason that finally persuaded me to write this book I would have to choose this one: the overwhelming majority of the Bartleby Industry reads the narrator of the story in a way that is not only different from mine but quite incompatible with mine. Every virtue I see in the man, they see as a vice; where I see his strength, they see his weakness; what I see as his genuine responsiveness, they see as his cold self-absorption. Some critics read the story as I do, but we are in a distinct minority. There are several reasons this should be so, and I think I understand at least some of them, but first I should like to present as fairly as I can the majority opinion.

Robert Weisbuch, who has said the Lawyer is Charles Dickens, refers to the Lawyer as "unnatural," "anti-natural," "lifeless," "self-satisfied," "pompous," and "rationalizing." The Lawyer "investigates Bartleby but refuses authentic emotional commitment in so doing," and "Bartleby rightly refuses to credit the Lawyer's false commitment." The Lawyer is guilty of "toadyism" and his final heartbroken outburst, "Ah Bartleby! Ah humanity!" is no more than "a someways hollow and unfeeling exclamation."[1] Another critic calls the Lawyer a "smug fool" who is "terribly unkind to a very sick man."[2] I had always thought of the Lawyer as a kind of stand-in for us, a figure we could identify with as we struggled to understand Bartleby. On the contrary, the narrator is "deficient in humanity and quite obtuse towards human beings." I must have had it backwards, for "surely this was Melville's intention: to have his reader *not* sympathize with the Lawyer, *not* to identify with him, *not* to put himself in the Lawyer's place" (*his* italics, not mine).[3] Another critic says, "The narrator attains new heights of vague sentimentality rather than a peak of awareness in his climactic and highly revealing sigh: 'Ah Bartleby! Ah humanity!'" This reader provides dismissive certainty in answering the question

> Who then is Melville's narrator? He is that sort of man one tends to find in high places: the snug man whose worldly success has convinced him that this is the "best of all possible worlds," and whose virtues cluster around a "prudential" concern for maintaining his own situation. The narrator can never fully understand or truly befriend Bartleby because the narrator is simply too complacent, both philosophically and morally, to sympathize with human dissatisfaction and despair.[4]

1. Robert Weisbuch, "Melville's 'Bartleby' and the Dead Letter of Charles Dickens," *Atlantic Double-Cross: American Literature and British Influence in the Age of Emerson* (Chicago: University of Chicago Press, 1986), pp. 44, 45–47.
2. David Shusterman, "The 'Reader Fallacy' and 'Bartleby, The Scrivener,'" *New England Quarterly*, 45 (March, 1972), 118–24, pp. 122–23.
3. Ibid., p. 121.
4. Allan Emery, "The Alternatives of Melville's 'Bartleby,'" *Nineteenth-Century Fiction*, 31 (1976), 170–87, pp. 186–87.

Still another reader tells us the Lawyer's commentary "rings with blasphemy" and demonstrates "grotesque manifestations of diseased conscience."[5]

Authority is the enemy here. In the extended quotation just above it is taken for granted that the "sort of man one tends to find in high places" is superficial and selfish. Worldly success is bad for the character. The Lawyer has to be bad, or he wouldn't be in an office on Wall Street. Hershel Parker tells us that "our ultimate opinion" of the Lawyer "is not contempt so much as bleak astonishment at his secure blindness. With a bitterer irony than the narrator is capable of, we murmur something like 'Ah narrator! Ah humanity!' In his self-consciously eloquent sequel, after all, the lawyer has merely made his last cheap purchase of a 'delicious self-approval.'" Parker maintains that when "this easy-conscienced" man speaks of kings and counsellors, "he is experiencing a comfortable, self-indulgent variety of melancholy"; when he quotes words from the Book of Job he does so "with prideful aptness," and "characteristically perverts them from profound lament to sonorous urbanity."[6]

This last feature of Parker's argument is interesting to me because it reminds me of the first time I read the story, at eighteen. I was overwhelmed by the discovery that Bartleby had died, and I didn't know that "With kings and counsellors" was a quotation from the Book of Job. The phrase "With kings and counsellors" seemed to me majestic and solemn and final. That "murmurred I" put a deep hush

5. William Bysshe Stein, "Bartleby: The Christian Conscience," in *Melville Annual 1965, A Symposium: "Bartleby the Scrivener,"* ed. Howard P. Vincent (Kent, Ohio: Kent State University Press, 1966), p. 107.

6. Hershel Parker, "The Sequel in 'Bartleby,'" in *Bartleby the Inscrutable: A Collection of Commentary on Herman Melville's Tale "Bartleby the Scrivener,"* ed. M. Thomas Inge (Hamden, Conn.: Archon Books, 1979), 159–65, pp. 163–64.

around it. But it never occurred to me that the man who said those words was "easy-conscienced" or "self-indulgent" or the sort of man who "characteristically perverts" a "profound lament to sonorous urbanity." The figure of Bartleby seemed so weird and funny and painful, his death at once inevitable and shocking, that I did not see it as an occasion for the man who was telling me about it to make a "last cheap purchase" of "delicious self-approval." I trusted that Lawyer.

Thirty years later, I still do. He seems to me extremely intelligent, whimsical and ironic, generous, self-aware, passionate, and thoroughly competent. But the views of Parker and Weisbuch are not at all idiosyncratic, and most critics seem to take it virtually for granted that Melville's lawyer-narrator is not very bright; he is humorless, selfish, blind, superficial, and bumblingly incompetent. Liane Norman says the reader "is jolted away from, after having connected himself with the Lawyer."[7] It must have been a very brief encounter, for the rupture occurs in the second paragraph when the Lawyer tells us how he likes to repeat the name of John Jacob Astor, and "unconsciously betrays himself." This, we are told, is an example of what another critic calls the "unconscious duplicity" of the Lawyer, for our narrator habitually tells us "far more of the truth than he intends."[8] Or, as Parker says, what we think of the narrator is "the product less of what he means to tell than what he unknowingly divulges." Critics poke holes in the Lawyer's words; they quite literally see through him. It is as if "Bar-

7. Liane Norman, "Bartleby and the Reader," *New England Quarterly*, 44 (March, 1971), 22–39, p. 26.

8. William B. Dillingham, "Unconscious Duplicity: 'Bartleby, The Scrivener,'" *Melville's Short Fiction, 1853–56* (Athens, Georgia: University of Georgia Press, 1977), p. 45.

tleby, The Scrivener" is not a story, it is a lie, and we should examine that lie, to find inconsistencies and contradictions in it. *We* are the lawyers here, and we have a hostile witness on the stand. We have to break him, and expose him for the inadequate and misguided man he really is.

Critics do not so much interpret the story as oppose the narrator's version to their idea of the "truth." The Lawyer "sees in his imagination the scrivener—but in reality himself—laid out, among uncaring strangers in a burial sheet."[9] This is a common feature of the critical readings; Bartleby is not really a person, he is a phantom crawling out of the unconscious dark pool of the narrator's repressed life. Another scholar says that "there is something cowardly" in the Lawyer's running from Bartleby "(assuming he is a real character, not merely a psychological projection)."[10] It is the kind of error Newton Arvin addresses in his commentary on *Moby-Dick* when he says that "taking everything 'spiritually' means not taking it spiritually enough" because the meanings of the work "would not be so wide-reaching and deep-plunging as they are if they were not embodied in a fable of which virtually every detail has a hard, concrete, prosaic, and even naturalistic substantiality."[11] To take Bartleby so "spiritually" makes him a "psychological projection" of the Lawyer instead of the wonderfully drawn character he is. We are told that the Lawyer "is not even 'acquainted'—socially or intimately—with what he himself really is" and that "his prudence and method insure self-deceit." His remark to the grub-man, "No, I was never socially acquainted with any forgers" becomes artificially italicized to "No, I was

9. Ibid., pp. 31–32.

10. Thomas Pribeck, "An Assumption of Naiveté: The Tone of Melville's Lawyer," *Arizona Quarterly*, 41 (Summer, 1985), 131–42, p. 142.

11. Newton Arvin, *Herman Melville* (New York: Viking, 1950), p. 168.

never socially acquainted with *any* forgers"—as if he were saying don't look at me, I never knew *any* of them—because the narrator himself "is a forger, a self-swindler." The Lawyer literally does not know what he says, and when he quotes the Book of Job, "the words carry an additional significance probably lost on the speaker."[12] Too wrapt up in his own concerns to understand Bartleby's he "likes to avoid trouble" and "finds it more convenient to duck the issue," and "in the end he still does not quite understand what has happened, nor why."[13] The Lawyer is a real scoundrel, for "in bragging that his associates consider him 'an eminently *safe* man,' the lawyer unwittingly suggests that inside knowledge about even financially shady deals would be secure with him."[14] Which is worse?—the "unwittingly" or his tidy silence about "shady deals"? He does not know where his words come from, and he accidentally lets us know he is a crook.

Not only do we know more about the Lawyer than he tells us, we know more about Bartleby than Bartleby himself tells us. He will not go home with the Lawyer because "he has seen something more in the offer than generosity and his refusal indicates his unwillingness to expose himself further to the kind of situation that has repeatedly victimized him."[15] When Bartleby says in the Tombs, "I know you," we are told he means "*I know you for what you are.*" The narrator's offer to take Bartleby home is something Bartleby sees through as an offer to provide "at best a *temporary* asylum,

12. Dillingham, "Unconscious Duplicity," p. 48.

13. Ethel Cornwall, "Bartleby The Absurd," *International Fiction Review*, 9 (Summer, 1982), 93–99, p. 93.

14. R. Bruce Bickley, Jr., *The Method of Melville's Shorter Tales* (Durham, N.C.: Duke University Press, 1979), p. 35.

15. Marvin Fisher, "'Bartleby,' Melville's Circumscribed Scrivener," *Southern Review*, 10 (January, 1974), 59–79, p. 74.

not brotherhood."[16] Our Lawyer "exhibits no evidence of contrition," and goes on "fatuously" bragging to the point that he "invites an association with Judas."[17] The Lawyer's sudden realization that Bartleby may be a "victim of innate and incurable disorder" becomes "the lawyer's utter perversion of the basic principles of Christianity."[18] Charity is a sign of weakness, for the Lawyer "is too afraid of creating a scene by throwing Bartleby out at the first sign of insubordination—as a stronger character would have done."[19] The "narrator's stuffy rhetoric depicts a cramped, diminished psyche" and demonstrates "finicky, anal behavior"; his language "quivers at every turn with erotic displacement" and "necrophilic tendencies."[20] In her widely praised book, *The Feminization of American Culture*, Ann Douglas says the Lawyer "is as barren as the scrivener he pities," and he "attempts to force the scrivener to express gratitude for his own benevolence." The Lawyer "is constantly trying to use Bartleby's plight to touch off his own emotions." He ruminates with "a kind of sadistic pity," and operates with "onanistic indulgence."[21]

Even those very few critics who defend the Lawyer do it half-heartedly. One of them says that "the narrator *is* good,

16. Cornwall, "Bartleby The Absurd," pp. 98–99.

17. Stein: "Bartleby: The Christian Conscience," p. 105.

18. Ibid., p. 108.

19. Cornwall, "Bartleby The Absurd," p. 95.

20. Lewis H. Miller, Jr., "Bartleby and the Dead Letter," *Studies in American Fiction*, 8 (Spring, 1980), 1–12, pp. 8–10. Reading such characterizations, one might hesitate to apply Milton R. Stern's verdict that "the critics who dismiss the narrator . . . are guilty of exactly the same sin of which they indict him": Stern, "Towards 'Bartleby the Scrivener,'" in *The Stoic Strain in American Literature*, ed. Duane J. MacMillan (Toronto: University of Toronto Press, 1979), p. 40.

21. Ann Douglas, *The Feminization of American Culture* (New York: Knopf, 1977), pp. 315–17.

is charitable—uncommonly so," but alas he is "all-too-human"; "Bartleby is a kind of personified, continual slap in the face," and the narrator is unable "to go on turning the other cheek forever."[22] The Lawyer is not Jesus Christ, and none of us is, so the story is "about every man's failure—or, more properly, inability to live by Christ's precepts in this imperfect, horological world of ours." Another critic cites some good qualities in the Lawyer, but concludes that the moral of the story is that we can't be our brother's keeper, for self-interest will finally prevail: "Only that reader who knows in his heart that in a similar situation he would have done more for some Bartleby than the lawyer did can claim to be free from 'the inherent selfishness of the human heart.'" As for "the rest of us," each may "find inscribed on his own heart the inexpungeable principle of self-interest—the first law of nature—which Melville intended to reveal here": "Melville sends a ghostly messenger seemingly from the dead not just to show that man would not be persuaded, but, given his common infirmities, he *cannot* be persuaded." Yes, "even a conscientiously good man like the lawyer is finally guided primarily by self-interest."[23]

Today, narrators are unreliable by definition. Fiction told in the first person is inherently deceptive. The great unreliable narrators—that dreadful man who tells us about *The Aspern Papers* or the much nicer but not altogether astute fellow who speaks to us in "The Real Thing"—represent not merely Henry James's wonderful play with perspective but also extreme examples of the condition of first-person narrative itself. This general notion is given a special class-conscious twist by the Bartleby Industry, for the Lawyer

22. Harold Schechter, "Bartleby The Chronometer," *Studies in Short Fiction*, 19 (Fall, 1982), 359–66, pp. 362, 365.

23. Walter Anderson, "Form and Meaning in 'Bartleby, The Scrivener,'" *Studies in Short Fiction*, 18 (Fall, 1981), 383–93, pp. 392–93.

seems to be wrong because he is a lawyer. The abundant misreadings of the "bad" Lawyer usually reveal an underlying animus toward the profession he represents. For example, one critic tells us the Lawyer is "an unreliable narrator" who "creates the story in order to justify his behavior toward Bartleby." The Lawyer "reduces Bartleby to the status of an object, a commodity." Bartleby's "alienation results from the dehumanizing experience of Wall Street, from the prison of his socioeconomic system." What is eating Bartleby is what is eating his co-workers: they cannot see that they constitute a class. Twentieth-century critics, however, can penetrate that nineteenth-century secret, for they see that "the lawyer reduces morality to a question of money," and he repeatedly offers money to Bartleby. Oppressor and oppressed are blind, both to themselves and to each other; the story is "one of the bitterest indictments of American capitalism ever published."[24]

Ann Douglas says the Lawyer's "sentimental illusion of brotherhood," is an "obfuscation of an essentially class situation, which the narrator demands as the price of his sympathy."[25] The narrator "unwittingly allows us to understand that these copyists are by small and futile oddities of behavior rebelling against the routinized and monotonous quality of their work."[26] In all of Melville's writings that exclude women characters, Melville "is interested primarily in questions of class: the clash between employer and employed, master and slave," and "Melville is dramatizing here the process by which an essentially mass sensibility transforms and assimilates the alien to its own needs."[27]

24. James C. Wilson, "'Bartleby': The Walls of Wall Street," *Arizona Quarterly*, 37 (Winter, 1981), 335–46, pp. 339, 346.

25. Douglas, *Feminization of American Culture*, p. 316.

26. Ibid., p. 316.

27. Ibid., pp. 298, 316.

In all these readings we are asked to see that the Lawyer represents "consumer capitalism"; we are asked to see, too, that the man refuses to recognize—or is simply incapable of recognizing—the political and economic forces that have made him what he is. Critic after critic tells us that the Lawyer cannot see his own complicity in the ruthless capitalist system and that we should read his every word as deliberate deception or hopeless failure. He is as blind as the poor Governess in "The Turn of the Screw."

But what if he is not? On the opening pages of his narrative the Lawyer spends considerable time and energy bragging about the very thing the critics say he cannot admit. And then the "eminently *safe* man" goes on to tell us that the advent of Bartleby in his life has forced him to question all his old rules. Modern socially conscious readers won't hear of it; they have their man. But they fail to reckon with the wonderfully dramatic quality of the story, the Lawyer's agonizing reappraisal of himself. He does not put it, back in 1853, in any of the language we use so wantonly more than a century later, but we watch him go weak in his knees with his prized "prudence" and "method" as he senses a rich and frightening world that his lifelong procedures have shut out. To see him as a representative of a class, an unwitting victim of a social and economic system, is not so much creative interpretation as it is obtuse paraphrase. One of the most interesting dramas in the story is the Lawyer's own helpless intuition that he is not adequate to the challenge of Bartleby, and never has been. His initial boasting about his virtues becomes his tortured exploring of them as weakness and failure. To read him out of his own brave story is to lose what is most lovely and spiritually generous about him.

It may be useful at this point to recall Bruce Franklin's identification of the story's source in Matthew 25:

The narrator fulfills the letter of Christ's injunction point by point: he offers money to the stranger so that he may eat and drink; he takes him in, finally offering him not only his office but also his home; when he sees that he is sick, he attempts to minister to him; he, alone of all mankind visits and befriends the stranger in prison.[28]

Franklin goes on, however, to read the narrator's fulfillment of the letter of Christ's injunction as a profound failure to fulfill the spirit of the law: the Lawyer

hardly fulfills the spirit of Christ's message: his money is carefully doled out; he tries to evict the stranger, offers his home only after betraying him, and then immediately flees from him in the time of his greatest need; it is his demands on the stranger which have made him sick; he visits the stranger in prison only once while he is alive, thus leaving him alone for several days before and after his visit, thus leaving him to die entirely alone.[29]

There is an odd prosecutorial tone here: Franklin is clearly out to get the Lawyer, and one might ask where the grudge comes from. The Lawyer appears only in the worst possible light, sometimes in an artificial light that makes things the opposite of what they would be in the clear light of day. Repeatedly, throughout the story, the narrator offers Bartleby money, at various times, in various ways, for various purposes, and at the end he gives the grub-man money to bring Bartleby good meals. Why, then, is his money "*carefully* doled out"? The instinctive reach for the wallet may look like a bribe, or a tip, but it is not careful doling out. Why does the narrator fail Bartleby "in the time of his greatest

28. Bruce Franklin, *The Wake of the Gods* (Stanford, Calif.: Stanford University Press, 1963), pp. 127–28.
29. Ibid., p. 128.

need"? When *is* Bartleby's "time of greatest need"? To say that the Lawyer does not visit Bartleby often enough, during his brief incarceration, penalizes generous activity; the Lawyer has tried to get Bartleby to come home with him to his own house. Is the Lawyer supposed to live in the Tombs with Bartleby? Franklin insists that the Lawyer "treats this strange being with contempt." With contempt? When Franklin concludes of the Lawyer that "all his charity is shown to be too little and too late," one can only wonder what is going to happen to the rest of us when we are called to the bar of judgment.

Seven years after he wrote about "Bartleby" in *The Wake of the Gods*, Franklin published an essay entitled "The Teaching of Literature in the Highest Academies of the Empire."[30] The essay includes the characterization of Herman Melville as "a consciously proletarian writer" who "wrote about the life of working people on ships and in factories and offices. He never went to college." Now this is Theodore Dreiser, maybe, or (with slight adjustments of the transcript) Frank Norris or Richard Wright. Franklin proposes that anybody who has "never done physical labor for a living" is "unqualified to teach Melville." We must "remould our ideas so that we can join the people and serve them." Here we have the agitprop ideas and language of the John Reed Clubs, the 1930s blueprints for "proletarian realism."

Six years later Franklin characterizes Herman Melville as "an artist whose creative imagination was forged in the furnace of proletarian experience, an artist who saw the world of nineteenth-century U.S. society and its commercial em-

30. Bruce Franklin, "The Teaching of Literature in the Highest Academies of the Empire," *College English*, 31 (March, 1970), 548–57.

pire through the eyes of a class-conscious worker."[31] Franklin goes on to say:

At this point in U.S. history, when you approach Melville as a proletarian artist, you expose yourself to the ridicule of the academic literary establishment, the professors who "earn" $15,000 to $40,000 a year by misrepresenting literature. To them, all great literature is without class content, for it "transcends" class struggle. Great literature exists to be appreciated—by them and their best students—for its greatness. That is, they reduce literature to a pleasant amenity of their own affluent existence. What is most vital and relevant about Melville is still suppressed and buried. For the Melville that is taught is a Melville redesigned in the image of the professors.

The animus expressed toward the Lawyer in "Bartleby," in 1963, has now carried over, thirteen years later, to those who study "Bartleby." The university itself is the "snug retreat," and the common denominator is class privilege. Franklin asserts that

the narrator of "Bartleby" is the man who converts these blank pieces of paper into the documents upon which capitalism rests: bonds, titles, and mortgages which declare that all the means of production, including that very paper mill, and all the products coming from it, including the pieces of paper themselves, do not belong to the people who produced them with their entire life's creativity, but instead are the private property of a handful of rich parasites.

Bartleby is really staging a sit-in, and "the narrator responds

31. Bruce Franklin, "Herman Melville: Artist of the Worker's World," in *Weapons of Criticism: Marxism in America and the Literary Tradition*, ed. Norman Rudich (Palo Alto, Calif.: Ramparts, 1976), 287–309, p. 287.

as the very essence of capitalist society, reducing all human relationships to money relationships."[32]

What is often only implied by "Marxist" critics, Franklin fully articulates: it is a deep hostility toward literary criticism itself and to those who practice it. Pervasive anxiety about Authority can find a sitting duck in a Master of Chancery whose employees address him "With submission, sir." Ginger Nut seems pretty cheerful, but he is twelve; Turkey is clearly alcoholic, Nippers is in a bad way, and Bartleby is dreadfully lost. Surely the Lawyer is where the buck should stop, the Boss of all this human misery. Anyone who invokes the human condition is a moral delinquent, blind to the real cash nexus and the perpetual warfare between unthinking capitalism and alienated labor.

But one might ask how it would help Bartleby if our Lawyer stopped being a lawyer. If he became a—a what?—a labor organizer? In 1853? Is there the slightest hint, anywhere in the story, that Bartleby would "prefer" the Lawyer to be other than what he is? Or that Bartleby could snap out of whatever it is that troubles him, and join his newfound progressive friend? Or what ramparts could they stand together? At the end, Bartleby says to the Lawyer, "I know you," and "I want nothing to say to you." Does he mean he knows the Lawyer is a lawyer and has nothing to say to such men? Or does he mean that he has nothing to say to anyone? Franklin says of the Lawyer that "it is his demands on the stranger which have made him sick." But Bartleby was sick when he first showed up at the door. The Lawyer remembers it as the first thing he noticed: "I can see that figure now—pallidly neat, pitiably respectable, incurably forlorn! It was Bartleby." The story says, and says everywhere, in direct contradiction to what the critics say, that this initial

32. Ibid., pp. 287, 300–301.

emphasis is correct: what is wrong with Bartleby is incurably wrong.

In my second chapter I considered some modern diagnoses of Bartleby as mentally ill. I should point out here that the very suggestion of it is anathema to socially conscious readers. All of them imply what some of them say explicitly: to see Bartleby the way the Lawyer sees him, as a victim of "excessive and organic ill," is itself a betrayal, a way of rationalizing class privilege. The Lawyer is a servant of decadent social arrangements, so he must himself be decadent. But what if he is not? What if Bartleby is unreachable by our very best impulses and our most enlightened social arrangements? The deepest question in the story is what you do with Bartleby. The deepest answer the story provides is that you can do nothing.

But that answer is a very painful one. Bartleby incurable? That thought seems to abandon him. We have to pin the blame on somebody. Let us pin it on the man who tells us. Who likes a man who says human pain is incurable? That thought is too much to bear—kill the messenger! But if we do not take the narrator seriously, we will never be able to take Bartleby seriously. If we listen to the narrator, we hear him telling us all along that looking at Bartleby has proved too difficult for him, too baffling and painful.

Richard Chase is right to remind us that "Melville had other models of style besides the great English authors" and that "one of these was the popular American rhetoric and oratory of his own time."[33] Remarking on the "most violent spirit of magniloquence" in nineteenth-century American public address, Chase points out that "oratory was one of the accomplishments of the folk hero. 'I can outspeak any man,'

33. Richard Chase, *Herman Melville: A Critical Study* (New York: Macmillan, 1949), p. 88.

was one of Crockett's boasts. An orotund native oratory, full of bombast, humorous mythology, and rough Americanism, emerged, as if by necessity, to express the tumultuous feelings of the people."[34] In *Mardi* Melville satirizes an orator when the travelers visit Washington and hear a speech by a western senator. With one hand the man hits his head, with the other he hits his hip; he roars like a wild animal: "I have said it! the thunder is flashing, the lightning is crashing! . . . Ha! ha! I grow hoarse but would mine were a voice like the wild bull's that I might be heard from one end of this great and gorgeous land to its farthest zenith!" In *Moby-Dick*, Father Mapple's sermon is not bombast, and it may indeed be what Chase calls it, "the high point of American oratory." But Melville describes Father Mapple himself, giving the sermon, rather like that senator in *Mardi:* Father Mapple "seemed tossed by a storm himself. His deep chest heaved as with a ground-swell; his tossed arms seemed the warring elements at work; and the thunders that rolled away from off his swarthy brow, and the light leaping from his eye, made all his simple hearers look on him with a quick fear that was strange to them." He behaves like the fire-and-brimstone preacher he is. He is also a man of high intelligence and great rhetorical skill; his sermon is immensely persuasive, an act of profound spiritual devotion and intellectual cogency. But Melville uses the standard metaphors and figures to establish Father Mapple's kinship with the great sermonizers and Fourth of July orators such as Daniel Webster, Theodore Parker, and Henry Ward Beecher—the big-time talkers.

Throughout Melville's work one finds him deeply interested in rhetorical performance. Redburn has "vague thoughts of becoming a great orator like Patrick Henry." In *Pierre* Melville speaks of "fiery revolutionary rhetoric" as

34. Ibid., p. 89.

"that great American bulwark and bore—elocution." Harrison Hayford points out that Melville's brother "Gansevoort was a Tammany Democrat who had won distinction as a campaign orator in 1844"; Melville undoubtedly had his brother's speeches for Polk in mind when he wrote Ahab's speech about needing a harpoon made of "young Hickory, baptised in fire and blood."[35] Melville is clearly using the figure of the traditional American orator, "the screamer," "the ring-tailed roarer" in Ahab's frenzied addresses to his crew.

This long and continuing interest in the art of public speaking can be heard everywhere in "Bartleby, The Scrivener." We do not accurately characterize the story if we say it is a plea to a jury. The Lawyer is not striding up and down before the box. I shudder to think how a critic could push to the point of absurdity this quality of the Lawyer's speech: this is the insanity plea, this is the court of last resort, Bartleby is the Lawyer's client, and we are the jury listening to the Lawyer pleading on Judgment Day. Or it is the Lawyer's own life on the line, and he is defending himself to us. One critic, John Stark, has noticed the Lawyer's insistence on "prudence" (his "first grand point" is "prudence," and he speaks of how Colt "imprudently" got excited, and he considers charity to be "a vastly wise and prudent principle"). "Prudence," Stark points out, is a recurrent word in Lemuel Shaw's decision in *Brown* v. *Kendall*. The Lawyer in "Bartleby" insists on "common usage and common sense." In Shaw's elaborate opinion, "common usage" is synonymous with "ordinary care," so our critic concludes that the narrator "is speaking as though he were protecting himself from legal liability." Stark notes that some readers have tried to

35. Harrison Hayford, "Melville and Hawthorne: A Biographical and Critical Study" (Diss., Yale University, 1945), p. 283.

show that "the lawyer represents Shaw," but objects to the identification because "the lawyer is unambitious, whereas Shaw nearly reached the pinnacle of the legal profession." Shaw "was both a successful attorney and the chief justice of an important state court," whereas the Lawyer works only in Chancery, "certainly not a prestigious calling. Melville may have changed details such as these to make it less obvious that he was portraying his father-in-law."[36] Stark characterizes the writing of fiction as a matter of "changing details" in order to make things "less obvious"; he asks us to think that "Shaw was great and influential because he grasped the policy implications of legal rules and decisions," but the Lawyer "does not understand the implications of his possible responses to Bartleby." The story grew out of Melville's intimate relationship with his father-in-law, and the story is explicitly and really about it. Melville "changed details" to hide it. Herman Melville's mind, in all these readings, is a Rube Goldberg machine: you put the real Lemuel Shaw in one end and the machine pops and sputters and coughs and finally spits out a disguised Shaw at the other end. Our critic concludes that "in 'Bartleby' Melville does not propose a better ethic" (than Shaw's in *Brown* v. *Kendall*), "but he clearly shows that Shaw's will not do." What a thing for a short story to "show!" Robert L. Gale asserts that Melville is "satirizing his pitying, charitable, successful, misunderstanding benefactor-tormentor."[37] The Lawyer repeatedly offers Bartleby money, creating the terrible dependence Melville eventually came to feel about his father-in-law's repeatedly bailing him out of financial trouble; the paternal

36. John Stark, "Melville, Lemuel Shaw, and 'Bartleby,'" in *Bartleby the Inscrutable*, ed. Inge, 166–73.

37. Robert L. Gale, "Bartleby—Melville's Father-in-Law," *Annali Instituto Universitaria Orientale*, 5 (Naples, 1962), p. 60.

figure's efforts are all misguided, for the wise man-of-the-world, the chief justice of the Commonwealth of Massachusetts, cannot stop his poor weak-eyed son-in-law the novelist from his course of suicidal ruin. Bartleby goes to his death after writing *Pierre*.

"Bartleby" is not a plea to a jury or even like a defense summary in a formal trial. But there is a profoundly spoken quality to the Lawyer's words. The Lawyer's voice is like the voices of other lawyers and preachers and politicians elsewhere in Melville's work. In "Bartleby" that spoken quality has a poignant, special effect. When I read it, I often wonder whether it really did come from a particular rhetoric book (say, Austin's *Chironomia*) that Melville happened to find, perhaps a book in his father-in-law's library, a chapter on how to talk to a jury. I do not think the story "Bartleby, The Scrivener" is based on any particular Aristotelian or Ciceronian model available to Melville in the homiletics texts of his day. Perhaps there is some original, but I doubt it. Still, I am reminded that for decades scholars thought Melville made up the hymn that precedes Father Mapple's sermon in *Moby-Dick*, until it was discovered to be a reworking of Psalm 18 in *The Psalms and Hymns of the Reformed Protestant Dutch Church in America.* After studying closely Melville's revision of the hymn, David H. Battenfeld says it "raises the question whether sources as yet undiscovered exist for many other key Melville passages—possibly even Father Mapple's sermon itself."[38] So with "Bartleby." The rhetorical maneuvers in the story are sufficiently elaborate to make it tempting to believe they come from somewhere. For a brief time I was vaguely haunted by the idea that Franklin's insistence on the

38. David H. Battenfeld, "The Source for the Hymn in *Moby-Dick*," *American Literature*, 27 (November, 1955), 393–96, p. 396.

centrality of Matthew 25 might point to a local context for Melville, in a sermon that Theodore Parker or someone might have given on the text "the least of these." Maybe so, but I have not found it.

The Lawyer is, however, quite a lawyer. He is given to what Herbert F. Smith calls "stunning examples of legal periphrasis." Smith maybe stretches a little too far when he asserts that Turkey and Nippers are *amici curiae* who "balance each other out like contrasting paragraphs on a contract," but the simile is faithful to the informing rhetoric of the story as a whole. Smith asserts that the word "prefer" is "exquisitely chosen" to suggest "'bearing before' or 'setting before' in the matter of consequential choice. It is also apposite to the situation of equity pleading as opposed to common law pleading."[39] Scholars may argue over how much we should see in the Lawyer's references to "'Edwards on the Will' and 'Priestley on Necessity,'" but Smith points out that "these very philosophic sounding titles are also perfectly appropriate as legal titles, especially for the purposes of equity pleading. All one need do is accept the pun on 'will' as 'testament' and 'necessity' in its legal sense, as cause in hardship. Both terms were common to equity pleading at the time of the writing of the story."[40] "The doctrine of assumptions" is the subject of "a bravura punning performance" in which "assume" and "assumption" occur a dozen times in two paragraphs.

In these figures of legal rhetoric we hear a man giving a formal speech and talking to himself. His legal vocabulary impedes what he wants to say, but it is all he has to say it with. A rich and impressive comedy lies in the disjunction

39. Herbert F. Smith, "Melville's Master in Chancery and His Recalcitrant Clerk," *American Quarterly*, 17 (1966), 734–41, p. 740.

40. Ibid., p. 740, n. 12.

between all the absurdly insistent legalisms and the naked human tragedy of Bartleby. The narrator's diction is highly inappropriate. Bartleby's simple declaration keeps making that abundantly clear to him. So, the more his legal vocabulary does not work, the more the narrator uses it; intensifying it is his way of raising his voice. He cannot answer "I prefer not to." So he retreats in a blizzard of legalisms. This "eminently *safe*" lawyer who tells us he "never addresses a jury" is helplessly trying to do exactly that, and the jury he addresses begins to look suspiciously like himself.

In "The Affidavit" chapter of *Moby-Dick* we hear the spoken quality in phrases such as "Grant it, since you cite it." The whole last paragraph is a send-up of pleading:

"if, by any possibility"
"if I shall ever deserve"
"if hereafter I shall do anything"
"if, at my death"

This little scherzo of legal language becomes the whole tone of "Bartleby." In page after page of "Bartleby, The Scrivener" we hear the Lawyer speaking to us in direct address:

"I waive"
"it is fit I make some mention"
"an adequate understanding of the chief character about to be presented"
"I must be permitted to be rash here"
"I should have stated before"
"here it must be said"
"arguing the probabilities *pro* and *con*"
"Imagine my surprise, nay, my consternation"
"It is common usage"
"Shall I acknowledge it?"

"Imagination will readily supply . . . but . . . let me say"
"I will briefly mention"

Throughout, he is a lawyer, and he is talking.

Another kind of speech that fascinates Melville is the Shakespearean soliloquy. He uses it again and again, as in the chapter "The Sphynx" in *Moby-Dick*, where we find an Elizabethan favorite, the soliloquy to the skull: "Speak, thou vast and venerable head," for "Thou has been where bell or diver never went; hast slept by many a sailor's side, where sleepless mothers would give their lives to lay them down." "O head! thou hast seen enough to split the planets and make an infidel of Abraham." Exploring Melville's various uses of this rhetorical device, F. O. Matthiessen points to one of Melville's most resonant modulations, in the "Sunset" chapter, Ahab muttering and moaning,

> Dry heat upon my brow? Oh! time was, when as the sunrise nobly spurred me, so the sunset soothed. No more. This lovely light, it lights not me; all loveliness is anguish to me, since I can ne'er enjoy. Gifted with the high perception, I lack the low, enjoying power; damned, most subtly and most malignantly! damned in the midst of Paradise! Good night—good night! (*waving his hand, he moves from the window.*)

We feel here Melville's immense capacity to rush into the very rhythms of Ahab's thought—something we always feel when Melville writes an extended speech for one of his characters; he has to get into the speaker's head and be the man. It is a furiously concentrated act that partakes simultaneously of distance and identification. There is poised reserve in the profound philosophical quality of the ideas, the careful rhetorical balance and the archaic diction; there is frantic fusion in those whimpering two words "No more."

This is no balmy idea. Ahab is right about himself: "gifted with the high perception," he does "lack the low, enjoying power." How could one describe Ahab more poignantly, or more accurately, than he has just described himself? At the mercy of immense psychological contradiction, which he sees with utter clarity, he is helpless to fix it. Split lividly, from top to toe, Ahab has a double sense of himself; he brings to full life all the energy in him that opposes his mad chase. We are told early on that "Ahab has his humanities." We believe it when we see how powerfully he can summon those humanities, here in "Sunset," or when he thinks of his wife and child and the Andes mowers asleep with their scythes rusting in the grass. Charles Olson says these passages relax the tensions of Ahab's hate and throw a veil of grief over the end of the book. Ahab's ferocious cunning about himself is joined to a great helpless sadness. The manic force of his self-assessments is chastened by intermittent bursts of longing and woe.

Ahab is mad, and the Lawyer in "Bartleby" is sane. But the two men have in common something that comes from deep in Melville's genius: an ability to imagine their other self—to put a little twist on Lionel Trilling's fine phrase, "the opposing self"—to marshal the intellectual and emotional strength to put forth immensely powerful feelings counter to the dominant feelings. Critics go wrong about the narrative voice of "Bartleby" when they fail to hear the Lawyer putting to himself his own most profound misgivings about himself. The critics turn his own misgivings against him, as if they came from outside him. But the Lawyer keeps recognizing what somebody else could say about him. Somebody? No, he, for he is answering himself in his own voice.

This self-division becomes a real problem for those who

have attempted to adapt the story to the movie or television screen. Alan Wade describes how he attempted to find pictures for words, some visual equivalent for the verbal texture of "Bartleby."[41] How does one show the Lawyer's habitual way of alternately saying yes and no? At first the writers thought two actors might be used, or one actor on a split screen. Wade says one might set the story up as a dialogue between two people. I think his idea is a good one, but because I disagree with him about certain details, the version below is my own. Note that I leave out a few of Melville's words, but I have not added any. Neither have I fooled with the pronouns, the alternating "I" and "you." It is the way the Lawyer's mind works; it is adversary pleading:

Lawyer #1: What shall I do? What shall I do? What ought I to do? What does conscience say I *should* do? . . . Rid myself of him, I must; go, he shall. But how?

Lawyer #2: You will not thrust him, the poor, pale, passive mortal—you will not thrust such a helpless creature out of your door? You will not dishonor yourself by such cruelty?

Lawyer #1: No, I will not, I cannot do that. Rather would I let him live and die here, and then mason up his remains in the wall.

Lawyer #2: What, then, will you do? For all your coaxing he will not budge. . . . surely you will not have him collared by a constable, and commit his innocent pallor to the common jail? And upon what ground could you procure such a thing to be done?—a vagrant, is he?

Lawyer #1: What! he a vagrant, a wanderer, who refuses to budge?

Lawyer #2: It is because he will *not* be a vagrant, then, that you seek to count him *as* a vagrant. That is too absurd.

Lawyer #1: No visible means of support: there I have him.

Lawyer #2: Wrong again.

41. Alan Wade, "From Text to Television: A Chamber Theatre Approach," *Literature in Performance: A Journal of Literature and Performing Arts*, 2 (April, 1982), 23–34.

I have tried to understand why Bruce Franklin turns his back on his own sound advice that "one must bear in mind while evaluating the narrator's behavior that he is continually defending himself from two possible accusations—that he is too hard-hearted and that he is too soft-hearted."[42] That is correct: the narrator would be "unreliable" if he became for us either a hard-hearted fiend or a soft-hearted patsy. But Franklin proceeds directly to read "straight" everything the narrator says: the "old Adam of resentment rose in me and tempted me concerning Bartleby," as if the narrator had not himself called it "resentment" and labeled it a temptation. Franklin, and the critics who follow his lead, write as if they were outside or above the narrator. But they are just telling us how the narrator describes himself. They make much of the Lawyer's reference to "mere self-interest" as if he had not himself said "mere," as if he had not himself said one would invoke it only "if no better motive can be enlisted," and that in doing so, "I strove to drown my exasperated feelings towards the scrivener." The Lawyer constantly scoffs at his own feelings and talks to himself: "Poor fellow, poor fellow! thought I, he don't mean any thing; and besides, he has seen hard times, and ought to be indulged." The critics hear him saying aloud and insultingly what he says silently: an example of how capitalism turns people into objects occurs when the Lawyer says to Bartleby that he is like "any of these old chairs." But the Lawyer is not talking to Bartleby, he is talking to himself: "Yes, Bartleby, stay there behind your screen, *thought I;* I shall persecute you no more; you are harmless and noiseless as any of these old chairs" (italics mine). And the Lawyer ends the sentence with the marvelously comic "in short, I never feel so private as when I know you are here." To believe the Bartleby Industry, the

42. Franklin, *Wake of the Gods*, p. 133.

Lawyer has no feeling for his clerks; he trivializes and demeans them. But the Lawyer really has a quite lively interest, a rather keen involvement, in all that his clerks do, and his gruffness masks his genuine affection for them. Standing in for us, he is not a saint or a devil; he is an affectionate man, fumbling a little, with his common sense and his generous instincts. He is too liable to the gossip and rumor of his colleagues—we know that because he tells us.

Two passages are usually quoted by those who denigrate the Lawyer. The first begins with the dire words: "Imprimis: I am a man who, from his youth upwards, has been filled with a profound conviction that the easiest way of life is the best. . . . All who know me, consider me an eminently *safe* man." I am always amazed to see how modern readers use these words to "prove" the narrator's shortcomings. He never addresses a jury, he is unambitious, doing "a snug business" and says that "I do not speak it in vanity" about things nobody in his right mind could speak about in vanity. Why would anyone brag about such cold small potatoes? Even if they were true—especially if they were true.

He invokes John Jacob Astor—with that sly characterization of Astor as "a personage little given to poetic enthusiasm," a man who endows the New York Public Library for "*useful* knowledge." It is Astor's will, and Melville had plenty of fun with it in *Mardi.* John Jacob Astor was a man known to everybody in 1853 as "the landlord of New York," "Old Skinflint," "Moneybags," "Scrooge." How is it possible to read this passage straight? The narrator says John Jacob Astor is "a name which, I admit, I love to repeat, for it hath a rounded and orbicular sound to it, and rings like unto bullion." Melville lays it on with a trowel: "I admit," "I love," "hath," "rounded and orbicular," "rings like unto"—you cannot avoid seeing the narrator sitting there savoring the words "John Jacob Astor" like marbles in his mouth. It is comedy. "Not unemployed," "I will freely add," "not insensible"—this is not the narrator's love of money; neither is it professional vanity or insensitivity to virtue. It is elaborate self-deflation, not puny self-love.

The second passage critics quote is the response to Bartleby's "passive resistance." The narrator tells himself he cannot fire Bartleby, "can get along with him," and "Yes. Here I can cheaply purchase a delicious self-approval. To befriend Bartleby; to humor him in his strange wilfulness, will cost me little or nothing, while I lay up in my soul what will eventually prove a sweet morsel for my conscience." Critic after critic cites this as irrefutable evidence of the Lawyer's dreadfulness. They maintain that only a moral idiot could say such a thing.

But that is true. They are right. Only a moral idiot could. That is just what the narrator tells us. He, not the critics, says "cheaply." He, not the critics, says "delicious." How could a man say "sweet morsel" straight? Look at the verbs—"purchase" and "lay up." The critics insist that to be Christian doesn't really involve personal sacrifice for the Lawyer. But, again, that is just what the Lawyer tells us: it will "cost me little or nothing." The self-irony here is crystal clear. And as soon as he has said it, he goes on, "But"—he could not keep up this bogus benevolence, it was like trying "to strike fire with my knuckles against a bit of Windsor soap," and what he explicitly calls "the evil impulse" mastered him. To take this as evidence of the Lawyer's bad character, words must lose their meaning and context lose its relevance. The Lawyer says to us that he was deceiving himself and letting Bartleby down. The critics shout back, no, you're deceiving yourself and letting Bartleby down.

Allan Silver recognizes the error. Of the "sweet morsel"

passage, Silver says, "the lawyer is not merely fatuous; it does not escape him that this test of Christian virtue is mild and easy."[43] Stanley Brodwin has a fresh insight into the Lawyer's last encounter with Bartleby in the Tombs. The Lawyer says, "The Egyptian character of the masonry weighed upon me with its gloom. But a soft imprisoned turf grew under foot. The heart of the eternal pyramids, it seemed, wherein, by some strange magic, through the clefts, grass-seed, dropped by birds, had sprung." Brodwin says "the thematic and connotative subtlety of the lines defies" our reading this passage "as yet another effusion of the lawyer's felicitous Victorian sentimentality": "Apart from the allusive imagery and poetic tone, the very syntax of that last line with its choppy, periodic form, phrase by phrase moving to the completing verb 'had sprung' tells us that Melville has joined his sensibility with his character's."[44] "Melville has joined his sensibility with his character's" is a stunning, intuitive leap: Brodwin sees that the Lawyer's language is too subtle and beautiful, too precise, to be a wash of bathos.

This is what Leo Marx saw biographically: the Lawyer—at his moment of greatest feeling—talks like Melville himself in a moment of profound self-examination. If the Lawyer were the man the critics tell us he is, we would surely have to finish the story with an awful thud. The sequel would be just another "sweet morsel." But that "not-unpleasing sadness" is exactly what the Lawyer opposes to the "overpowering stinging melancholy" he suddenly feels about Bartleby.

What the Lawyer actually says, in all his self-denigra-

43. Allan Silver, "The Law and the Scrivener," *Partisan Review*, 48 (1981), 409–22, p. 414.

44. Stanley Brodwin, "To the Frontiers of Eternity: Melville's Crossing in 'Bartleby, the Scrivener,'" in *Bartleby the Inscrutable*, ed. Inge, 174–96, p. 188.

tions, is so natural—we all do it, in an attempt to distance difficult experience, to label it as well-it-can't-be-helped, let's-be-done-with-it. To prove that the Lawyer is an unreliable narrator the critics merely quote what he says all along, as a precaution against being unreliable:

> my vanity got the better of my pity
>
> something from within me upbraided me
>
> a certain squeamishness, of I know not what, witheld me
>
> I strangely felt something superstitious knocking at my heart . . . forbidding me to carry out my purpose, and denouncing me for a villain

Why do we need to be harder on the Lawyer than he is on himself? I hear him speaking in every line. His training, his practice, his whole life is backing up on him. The narrator defines himself as a professional man: he believes in what he does, believes that what he does is who he is. In the last paragraphs he is reaching for some explanation, some reason, anything to help. He knows it cannot really work. He explicitly says to us, "I hardly know whether I should divulge one little item of rumor." He "could never ascertain" its basis and "cannot now tell" us "how true it is." He will only "briefly mention it." With all that stammering qualification, he tells us the "vague report" of the Dead Letter Office. His heart needs it, his worn-out and famished brain is hungry for it. Critics are extremely suspicious of him here, and they indict him with Victorian cliché. They will not be sidetracked; they want to get on to Chancery and Wall Street, where the real evil of the world lies. No shrewd observer of the human animal believes in its genuine goodness. But Melville really does ask us questions about kindness, about love, about what we can fix and what we cannot. What happens when you run into something you cannot explain and cannot remedy? Where is your humanity then?

Robert Weisbuch sees the Lawyer not only as Dickens but also as Melville's parody of "the typical Dickensian villain." But the typcial Dickensian villain looks for weakness to gain power over it, to get an advantage. When the Lawyer sees Bartleby's impoverishment laid bare, he cries out, "His poverty is great; but his solitude, how horrible! Think of it." This is exactly what the typical Dickensian villain cannot do: he cannot "think of it" in sympathetic terms. The Lawyer searches and speculates and probes his own soul; he tries to find his own self-interest and negligence and indifference—all of which vices the critics quote as if the Lawyer were guilty of them, when the truth is that his own negligence is exactly what worries him. The Lawyer, driven crazy by self-doubt, by the most rigorous and extensive self-examination of which he is capable, is seen by the critics as a fool who never questions anything. The critics say that to listen to the authentic voice of the Lawyer is to be tricked into relaxing one's deepest convictions about what is wrong with the world. Bartleby cannot bring us to "a certain hopelessness."

Yes he can. The agony of the story lies in the Lawyer's genuine and terrified account of how the "forlornness of Bartleby grew and grew to my imagination." All through the story the Lawyer is asking what it is that has so damaged Bartleby. At the end, the Lawyer tentatively proposes an answer, hemmed in with qualifications. Many critics find fault with that final explanation. One critic says that "Melville did not let well enough alone" and that "the final long paragraph is the flaw that mars the perfection of the whole."[45] I sym-

45. Charles G. Hoffmann, "The Shorter Fictions of Herman Melville," *South Atlantic Quarterly*, 52 (July, 1953), 420.

pathize with Kingsley Widmer's instinct to preserve a mystery "against which all reason is helpless," but he speaks for the critical consensus when he finds that the final page leaves Bartleby "charitably patronized in memory," in a "thick Victorianism" which marks the Lawyer's "moralizing and rationalizing failure to understand Bartleby."[46]

The last page brings to a focus two of the central problems in the story: the nature of Bartleby's illness and the Lawyer's capacity to understand it. The "sequel" does help to explain certain details that go before it—for example, as Bruce Bickley says, when the Lawyer asks Bartleby to run an errand to the post office, that is "probably the last place, if the rumor is correct, that Bartleby would ever want to go."[47] But nobody seems to take seriously the Dead Letter Office as an explanation for what went wrong with Bartleby; most critics tell us that the rumor is a boomerang, and it flies right back to the Lawyer, showing us what is wrong with him.

Consider the quiet beauty of the Lawyer's response to the grub-man's question, "Won't he dine to-day, either? Or does he live without dining?"

> "Lives without dining," said I, and closed the eyes.
> "Eh!—He's asleep, ain't he?"
> "With kings and counsellors," murmured I.

Why not end it there? Melville drops down a few lines and says, "There would seem little need for proceeding further in this history"—and maybe he is right. Does the final paragraph really add anything? Indeed, how could one add anything equal to those poignant words?

In his very shrewd preface to "The Turn of the Screw,"

46. Kingsley Widmer, *The Ways of Nihilism: A Study of Herman Melville's Short Novels* (California State Colleges, 1970), pp. 118–19, p. 119.

47. Bickley, *Method of Melville's Shorter Tales*, p. 42.

Henry James proposes the necessity of releasing the reader from "weak specifications." James discusses ghost stories, objecting to their usual superfluity of atmospheric effects—clanking chains and howls in the night. James insists these are not nearly so frightening as what a reader will supply from the depths of his own mind. "Bartleby" is not exactly a ghost story, but James's principle applies: what we bring to Bartleby might be more eerie and convincing than the Dead Letter Office and deeper than anything Melville could say. Whatever our author puts in is a "weak specification" compared to what we ourselves provide.

In trying to find a rhetorical model for the Lawyer's speech, I unearthed what seemed to be a source for the final paragraph. At the end of Merton M. Sealts, Jr.'s *Melville's Reading: A Check-List of Books Owned and Borrowed*, I read, down in the W's, item number 546:

Warren, Samuel. The Moral, Social, and Professional Duties of Attorneys and Solicitors . . . New York, Harper, 1849.[48]

It was listed in the original inventory as "1 Warren's Duties"—which made me think it was a fairly standard text, "Warren's Duties" as, say, "Murray's Grammar" in *Moby-Dick*. At the beginning of Warren's warnings to his prospective lawyers, he speaks of a deceased client in much the same tone, and with many of the same words, that the Lawyer uses in his last paragraph about Bartleby:

Your unfortunate client shall receive no effectual redress: perhaps none at all. He may be beyond the reach of all earthly redress: he may be moldering in his grave, into which he descended, not

48. Merton M. Sealts, Jr., *Melville's Reading: A Check-List of Books Owned and Borrowed* (Madison: University of Wisconsin Press, 1966), p. 104.

knowing, poor soul, that he was leaning on a broken reed, in relying on his professional adviser's competence to arrange his affairs; that his affectionate and just purposes were destined to be all defeated! The "dull cold ear of death" can not hear of a will that is mere *waste paper* . . . of a widow and orphans reduced to destitution, while property, righteously destined for them, is being, through your instrumentality, enjoyed by a comparative stranger, or even by the bitterest enemy of your dead victim! Language, gentlemen, is not strong enough adequately to stigmatize . . .

Warren's last phrase made me remember the Lawyer's saying "I cannot adequately express the emotions which seize me." Warren's italicized "waste paper" might have given Melville the idea for the "Dead Letters"; we hear an exact echo of Warren's "moldering in his grave" in Melville's "moulders in the grave." Warren is saying to prospective lawyers that a man they should have taken care of is now "beyond the reach of all earthly redress," a "poor soul," and his property never reaches those for whom it was intended. Just so: Melville's "bank-note sent in swiftest charity" never gets there, and the ring never reaches "the finger it was meant for." Warren is filling up his young apprentice lawyers with fantasies that are clearly echoed in the images of Melville's elderly lawyer. I was particularly struck by Warren's speaking of "some one suddenly seized with mortal illness, or who has suffered some dreadful accident, hurrying him to a premature death-bed," someone (in Warren's own italics) "suddenly bidden, by the Supreme Disposer of events, to *turn his pale face to the wall*."[49]

But there are other possible sources for Melville's Dead Letter Office in the newspapers he read, and the imagery is

49. Samuel Warren, *The Moral, Social, and Professional Duties of Attorneys and Solicitors* (New York: Harper, 1849), p. 114.

as compelling as any in "Warren's Duties."[50] Hershel Parker discovered "Dead Letters—By a Resurrectionist," which appeared in September 1852 in the *Albany Register*, a story that describes in detail "all the thousand varied emotions, sympathies and expressions that go to make up 'correspondence'" which are "converted into lifeless, meaningless trash."[51] Parker concludes that "accumulating evidence suggests there was a vogue of Dead Letter articles about the time 'Bartleby' was written."

We may discover where Melville found his Dead Letter Office, but not how he used it, and that is what we really want to know. There is something wrong with Bartleby, so badly wrong that he dies of it. He does not expound a doctrine, like "Civil Disobedience," or shake his fist at the sky in protest of cosmic injustice, or hang his head about the difficulties of being a "writer." He starves to death. What the Lawyer says about the Dead Letter Office is the Lawyer's way of answering for himself what we want to know, too. One critic accuses the Lawyer of "inventing" the Dead Letter Office as a "sop to his conscience." That seems to me a desperate confusion about the very status of fiction. It reminds me of a student of mine who read Faulkner's "Delta Autumn" in a similar way. The student attributed Ike McCaslin's "racist" ideas to William Faulkner (who in some measure shared them). But the young woman who delivers a rebuff to Faulkner's racism seemed to the student to walk into the story all by herself, without any help from Faulkner: "Old man, have you lived so long and forgotten so much that

50. See John Middleton, "A Source for Bartleby," *Extracts*, 15:9, for a brief item in the Pittsfield *Sun*, February 17, 1853. See, too, George Monteiro, "Melville, 'Timothy Quicksand,' and the Dead-Letter Office," *Studies in Short Fiction*, 9 (Spring, 1972), for an article in the *New England Magazine*, 1831.

51. Parker, "The Sequel in 'Bartleby,'" pp. 159–60.

you don't remember anything you ever knew or felt or even heard about love?"[52] My student could see that Faulkner wrote Ike's speeches, but saw the young woman as a product of "our" enlightened world, not Faulkner's darkly prejudicial one.

Similarly, against what can we measure the Lawyer's report about the Dead Letter Office? Everything we know about Bartleby comes from the Lawyer. Is this a soul-comforting fabrication, or was he wrong before, and did he tell us a lot of lies back there? Does the Lawyer fade in and out of the truth? Which parts of his testimony should we "privilege"?

The elaborate hedging the Lawyer uses to introduce the rumor tells us that he himself wonders whether it is true. But it is not true or false to some world outside the Lawyer's mind. The question is the adequacy, not the veracity, of the last paragraph. Even if the Dead Letter Office career of Bartleby is "true," something was wrong with Bartleby when he went there. In telling us about it, the Lawyer asks us to "conceive a man by nature and misfortune prone to a pallid hopelessness." Bartleby was that way when he walked in, not when he got kicked out. The Dead Letter Office was the perfect place for him. The "business" there was "fitted to heighten" what already was amiss. As Milton R. Stern powerfully argues, the Dead Letter Office "keeps the focus exactly where Melville wants it—on the effect of Bartleby's condition, not on the cause of it."[53]

Something terrible happened in the Melville household on September 11, 1867. Malcolm, 18, the elder of Melville's

52. The line is said virtually word for word by Bea Richards to Spencer Tracy in the movie *Guess Who's Coming to Dinner?*

53. Stern, "Towards 'Bartleby the Scrivener,'" p. 35.

two sons, was doing well, paying his own way, working in an insurance office run by Allan Melville's brother-in-law. Malcolm had held his promising position for some months. Outgoing and high-spirited, he was rather liable to dreams of glory; too young to have served in the Civil War, he was much impressed by family stories of his cousins' heroism in battle. He joined a volunteer military outfit and relished dressing up in its splendid uniform with brass buttons. He carried around a pistol with a ball in it; at work the clerks told him to stop brandishing it about. Each night he kept it, loaded, under his pillow while he slept. To the dismay of his parents he had begun to go out on the town with the cadets in his company, drinking and carousing until all hours. Finally, after repeated warnings, his father took his house key away from him. Nevertheless, as Leon Howard tells it, on the night of September 10 Malcolm "remained out until three o'clock while his mother, after the house was locked as usual at eleven, stayed up to let him in, remind him of his responsibilities, and kiss him good night."[54] He was never seen alive again. Early next morning he answered when he was called to, but he did not come to breakfast. At the table his father said they should just let him sleep, let him be late for work, where he would have to take the consequences and perhaps learn a lesson. But as the day wore on, Malcolm failed to respond to knocks at his door. His mother found it locked. All afternoon the family worried. Finally Herman came home from work, broke down the door, and there they found him "still in his night clothes with his pistol firmly grasped in his right hand and a bullet hole in his temple."[55]

The next day, the coroner's jury ruled it a "suicide under

54. Leon Howard, *Herman Melville: A Biography* (Berkeley: University of California Press, 1951), p. 285.

55. Ibid., p. 285.

temporary insanity of mind," and so it was reported in the newspapers. A few days later, September 16, the verdict was changed (perhaps through the intervention of Melville) to "accidental self-destruction." The parents were horribly affected; Herman felt it was his fault for being too strict, and Lizzie felt it was her fault for being too indulgent.[56] Malcolm was buried in his company's uniform. Herman wrote to his brother-in-law, John Chipman Hoadley, "I wish you could have seen him as he lay in his last attitude, the ease of a gentle nature. Mackie never gave me a disrespectful word in his life, nor in any way ever failed in filialness." And, to a niece, he wrote that Mackie was "always obliging and affectionate" in "his whole nature and conduct."

It is extremely difficult to re-create a tragedy like this with any kind of integrity. You end up seeing what you want to see. But, as Leon Howard says, from this time onward Malcolm's death was never far from his parents' minds, especially as they helplessly watched the restless wanderings of their younger boy. At times Stanwix seemed to be parodying his father's career, as he had described it in *Typee* and *Omoo.* Stanny was all over the globe, jumping ship to become a beachcomber. In years to come he would show up in Kansas, New Orleans, the Indian Nation, Havana, various Central American cities—bumming about and doing odd jobs, spending a few months practicing dentistry and two years herding sheep. Howard says that "every decision and worry involving Stanwix during these years was related, in his parents' minds, to the fate of Malcolm."[57] In February 1886, after a long illness, Stanwix died alone in a San Francisco hospital.

A few critics have suggested that the sins of the children

56. Tyrus Hillway, *Herman Melville* (Boston: Twayne, 1979).
57. Howard, *Herman Melville*, p. 293.

should be visited on the father. Clearly, it was not an easy job to live with the man who had written *Moby-Dick* and *Pierre*. Everyone in the family agreed that he was hard to live with while he was writing. But all through the nervous crotchets and irritabilities, Melville continually expressed underlying devotion for his family. In London, in 1849, passing up an invitation from the Duke of Rutland to come visit Belvoir Castle, Melville wrote to Lizzie, "Would that One I know were here. Would that the Little One too were here." Malcolm was "growing all the time," and his father felt "like chartering a small boat and starting down the Thames instanter for New York." When Malcolm was eleven, his father wrote to him (September 16, 1860), "I suppose you have followed out on the map (or my *globe* were better—so you get Mama to clean it off for you) the route from Boston to San Francisco. The distance, by the straight track is about 1600 miles; but the ship will have sailed before she gets there nearer 18 or 2000 miles. So you see it is further than from the apple-tree to the big rock."[58] Edwin Haviland Miller takes two passages from this letter to Malcolm as proof that the father was mean-spirited and irresponsible. Miller reads Melville's advice to his son as intensely disagreeable: "I hope that you have called to mind what I said to you about your behaviour previous to my going away. I hope that you have been obedient to your mother, and helped her all you could, & saved her trouble. Now is the time to show what you are—whether you are a good, honorable boy, or a good-for-nothing one." Miller calls this "the kind of gratuitous advice that no son deserves."[59]

58. *The Letters of Herman Melville*, ed. Merrell R. Davis and William H. Gilman (New Haven: Yale University Press, 1960), p. 201.

59. Edwin Haviland Miller, *Melville* (New York: George Braziller, 1975), p. 302.

It does not read that way to me, given the way fathers wrote to sons in 1860, given the context in which it appears. But Miller and I differ drastically on the context. He thinks the forty-one-year-old father "might at least have spared his eleven-year-old son" the following story about a shipboard accident:

> Well, all at once, Uncle Tom saw something falling through the air, and then heard a thump, and then,—looking before him, saw a poor sailor lying dead on the deck. He had fallen from the yard, and was killed instantly.—His shipmates picked him up, and carried him under cover. By and by, when the time could be spared, the sailmaker sewed up the body in a peice [*sic*] of sail-cloth, putting some iron balls—cannon balls—at the foot of it. And, when all was ready, the body was put on a plank, and carried to the ship's side in the prescence [*sic*] of all hands. Then Uncle Tom, as Captain, read a prayer out of the prayer-book, and at a given word, the sailors who held the plank tipped it up, and immediately the body slipped into the stormy ocean, and we saw it no more.

Miller says, "Melville evidently never thought for a moment of the effect such a tragedy would have upon a youth whose father was now far away from Pittsfield aboard a ship where death might overtake him at any time."[60] Miller finds this an especially awful story for the eleven-year-old Malcolm, given the way the boy looks in a photograph of that time. (I have examined the photograph, and Malcolm looks just fine to me—though Stanwix, I'm afraid, does not.) The story of the sailor's death strikes me as just what kids would want to hear. We think our fathers are immortal, and we love to hear about the dangers they have passed through, the bloodier the better.

60. Ibid.

Melville writes to his children with great love and care. On this same voyage he writes to Elizabeth, seven,

> I hope you take good care of little
> FANNY
> and that when you go on the hill, you go this way:
> [here Melville sketches in a funny little drawing of a hill with two trees at the top and two little girls at the bottom, with hats on]
> that is to say, hand in hand.
> By-by
> Papa[61]

In London, in November of 1849, he finds himself alone in his hotel room on Saturday night; his mind turns to the thought of his brother Gansevoort, now dead, "writing here in London, about the same hour as this—alone in his chamber, in profound silence—as I am now." The death of his brother, in this great city far from home, the brother who at the time of his death had been finding an English publisher for *Typee*, made Melville feel so mournful that the rest of the night became "one continuous nightmare till daylight." The nightmare resonated again a few days later, when he moved on to Paris and visited the Hôtel de Cluny, the basis for that great passage on Thermes in *Moby-Dick*, Ahab's nightmare of mutilation.

Melville was peevish about his coffee and the consistency of his oatmeal; he was subject to irrational tempers. We should not minimize the extraordinary damage that the composition of *Moby-Dick* and *Pierre* did to his mental and emotional well-being. Neither should we ignore the abundant evidence of the warm and thoughtful man he was. Julian Hawthorne changed his mind about a great many things,

61. *Letters*, p. 205.

but when he was a boy, he said he loved Melville as much as his own father. There is something quite touching in Melville's relations with his brothers, especially the lifelong devotion to Tom. We know about his most sympathetic relationship with his father-in-law. He began his greatest book, and ours, by asking us to call him Ishmael; he ends that book as "another orphan." Throughout his life and work, family is his profoundest yearning. After Malcolm's death, Melville writes to his niece: "We have been getting new photographs made from two tin-types—one representing him in his ordinary dress, and the other in the regimental one. They have been reproduced (on a somewhat enlarged scale) much better than we could have anticipated."[62]

In her book *Dickens and Melville in Their Time*, Pearl Chester Solomon discusses the relationship between "Bartleby, The Scrivener" and "A Christmas Carol." The two stories are not much alike, but they are both about "master and workman in a great commercial city" and it "is a relationship which is fundamental to the nineteenth century, almost as important as that of father and son." The Lawyer and Bartleby are not father and son, but they "*do* exist as a father and son of a certain kind—a father and son who do not know one another, and who cannot communicate with each other; unable to teach, unable to learn; whose only gestures of mutual recognition are withdrawal, dismissal, and death."[63]

Richard Chase sees the relationship between them in these terms, too, when he finds at the "deepest symbolic level of the story" that "Melville is as much the lawyer, the man of action, aggression, and authority, as he is Bartleby. That is to say, Melville is as much the father as the son. For we have

62. Ibid., p. 229.

63. Pearl Chester Solomon, *Dickens and Melville in Their Time* (New York: Columbia University Press, 1975), pp. 8–9, 13.

indeed once more come upon Melville's central theme: the relationship between the father and the son and their failure or success in achieving the atonement, in redeeming each other."[64] This "deepest symbolic level" is in all of the "three B's"—"Bartleby," "Benito Cereno," and "Billy Budd"—in which we watch the efforts of "fathers" to save their "sons" from hurting themselves. But so radically and disastrously unsuccessful are the fathers that all the sons die: the Lawyer cannot save Bartleby, Captain Delano cannot save Don Benito, and Captain Vere cannot save Billy. The Lawyer says he is a man who "seldom indulge[s] in dangerous indignation at wrongs and outrages," and Delano is "not liable, except on extraordinary and repeated incentives, and hardly then, to indulge in personal alarms." Captain Delano tells Don Benito that "the past is passed; why moralize upon it?" and asks him to "See, yon bright sun has forgotten it all, and the blue sea, and the blue sky; these have turned over new leaves." The Lawyer says to Bartleby of the Tombs, "And see, it is not so sad a place as one might think. Look, there is the sky, and here is the grass." But Don Benito turns away from Delano, saying that the trade winds "waft me to my tomb"; Bartleby says to the Lawyer, "I know where I am," and "I want nothing to say to you."

Edwin Haviland Miller argues that the story of the Lawyer and Bartleby is about the "familial bond between them" and the "antagonism of father and son." When Bartleby refuses to eat, we should see it as his attempt "to punish the lawyer, the nurturing parent," for "there is no more effective and unsettling tactic than this for a child to get even, to cause parental anxiety and guilt."[65] Bartleby seems to be engaged in one of those Games People Play, this one called You'll Miss Me When I'm Gone. It works, as the Lawyer's final

64. Chase, *Herman Melville*, p. 148.
65. Miller, *Melville*, p. 264.

paragraph shows. Mr. Miller expresses virtually the same idea that guided George Bluestone when he made a film version of the story:

> I wrote a kind of interior monologue for Bartleby in which he felt a spiraling resentment of, and resistance to, the Lawyer. Bartleby was thinking, "If he's going to make such a holy row, I'll really show him a thing or two about passive resistance." In the prison scene, Bartleby was thinking, "You failed me and I'm going to punish you by dying," etc.[66]

"Spiraling resentment," "show him a thing or two about passive resistance," "punish you by dying, etc."—all these phrases are unfortunate. They trivialize Bartleby. They juvenilize him. Miller creates a caricature of a petulant child trying to get even.

But if Bartleby is not really a son, the Lawyer feels profoundly fatherly toward him. Or, one could say, not being Bartleby's actual father, the Lawyer feels about Bartleby with special intensity; this "rather elderly man," "snug" and "safe," has missed out on any generative role. His vital energy has gone into his profession instead of a family. He has had to fall back on the good opinion of John Jacob Astor. But now, at long last, he has a "son." All we have to do, to see it this way, is to take literally all those critics' descriptions of the Lawyer as "paternalistic." Régis Durand says Melville's obsessive search for the father frequently involves "the translation of the image of the father into a conventional or institutional figure, say a captain, a hero, or a god."[67] Or, one might add, a Lawyer.

66. George Bluestone, quoted in *Melville Annual 1965*, ed. Vincent, p. 50.

67. Régis Durand, "'The Captive King': The Absent Father in Melville's Text," in *The Fictional Father, Lacanian Readings of the Text*, ed. Robert Con Davis (Amherst: University of Massachusetts Press, 1981), 48–72, p. 54.

Some critics suggest that our unreliable narrator fails to see how fast he is going down a one-way street. His feeling rushes out toward Bartleby—but what he really wants is some acknowledgment, some love in return. It comes, of course, years later, when Billy Budd says, "'God bless Captain Vere.'" Only in the very last chapter of this sustained story of father and son does the son reply, in an excruciating phrase. And it is the father's word itself that condemns the son to death. Newton Arvin goes so far as to suggest that

> Billy might *be* his son, for Billy is a foundling and one in whom noble descent is as evident as in a blood horse; and the aristocratic Captain Vere, a bachelor, "was old enough to have been Billy's father." Whatever took place in the stateroom between the ideal father and the ideal son, its effect was indeed sacramental, an effect of the purest unction and the most complete reconcilement.[68]

Arvin sees "Billy Budd" as a summation of all the previous incarnations of the father-son story. "Ishamel, in the end, after so long a banishment, had been taken back to his father's heart." It is a story Melville could not stop writing, so great was the pain of it.

Notice the three adverbs in the sentence "'I prefer not to,' he respectfully and slowly said, and mildly disappeared." The first adverb, "respectfully," goes with that phrase repeated by the senior scrivener, "With submission, sir." In Bartleby's mouth it sounds like "haughtiness." There is a funny hum about "respectfully." Then, "slowly"—we watch him go, and we see that the "slowly" is part of the eerie, unhurried stateliness of the man. And "mildly" is a shocker—how do you *mildly* disappear? "Mildly" is genuinely haunt-

68. Arvin, *Herman Melville*, p. 299.

ing. Various forms, both funny and ghostly, of the word "mild" play through the story. (Melville speaks more than once of the "mildness" of the white whale, and "mild" will become a leitmotif of *The Confidence Man*.) Together, the three adverbs create a leisurely little excursion into the uncanny.

What kind of narrator do we infer from the three adverbs? If you take the view of the critical majority, the Lawyer would be constitutionally incapable of putting the words together. But he speaks this way throughout the story. Most critics say he means more than he says, "unwittingly." Those three adverbs seem to me pretty witting. If this is what we mean by Victorian sentimentality, we are very unlucky to have lost it. A man who says "respectfully," "slowly," and "mildly" like that stakes a claim on our best attention.

The last thing I have to say concerns the story's comedy. Most critics nod at it politely and then go on about their somber business. But the comic quality is one of our chief delights in reading "Bartleby." The anguish in the story is real, of course, and I know of no other word than "anguish" to use. When I read the solemn scholarship, however, I do not find much recognition of the hilarity on the way to the anguish. Perhaps both emotions, the tragedy and comedy, are blinked: failure to deal with one guarantees failure with the other. On the last page of the story you hear a heart breaking, but you would never guess it from those critics who laboriously put on their heavy scholarly armor and say, "Can't fool me—I know that's not genuine emotion, I know that's Victorian gush!" Maybe an inability to mourn goes with an inability to laugh. But one of the greatest comic lines I have ever read—sublimely comic, a line that made me laugh out loud when I first read the story as a freshman, a line that still makes me laugh as a professor—comes when the Lawyer-narrator is trying to get Bartleby to consider other vocational options and asks him, "How then would going as a companion to Europe, to entertain some young gentleman with your conversation,—how would that suit you?" When I first read that question in my freshman dorm, I pictured the "young gentleman" and Bartleby on a slow boat to China, or a luxury liner to France. I saw the young gentleman say, "Deck tennis, anyone?" and I saw Bartleby wrapped up in a blanket in a deck chair, staring at the horizon: "I prefer not to." The line goes faster and differently for me now—I don't picture them on the deck of a ship—but one thing has always been true: it is wonderfully funny. The way we encounter Bartleby is analogous to the way the narrator encounters him. Bartleby throws you back on yourself in sputtering exasperation and self-justifying. You cannot "fix" Bartleby, so one thing you do is talk about yourself—it's not *my* fault, *I'm* a good guy, don't look at *me*.

Richard Chase is right once again when he says the story "is a starkly simple tale told with great economy of metaphor and symbol." There is no room in it for endlessly proliferating symbology, as in *Moby-Dick*. Melville creates something intentionally bare, dingy, and drab. Chase says "Bartleby" has "a kind of simplicity at once nakedly tragic and wistfully comic." That "at once" is crucial; comedy is not the fringe benefit the critics pass right by. No, the comedy is there "at once" with all the pain, chastening it and transforming it. Chase says, "Melville, we must remember, was a humorous writer, as well as a lyric and epic writer." His humor can be "hearty, jovial, and broad"; it can be "lyrical and heroic"; it can be a "flowing stream of fantasy, alternately gay, grim, festive, erotic, regretful, and sad"; it is often "spare, light-footed, buoyant, and savage."[69]

Robert E. Abrams examines Henri Bergson's theory of

69. Chase, *Herman Melville*, p. 67.

"the laughable" in "automatism." Abrams shrewdly points out that Bergson has been popularly misunderstood to suggest that "robotism" is the essential element in the comic. Bergson's real insight was in "the comic dissonance of automatism within the human" so that the funny and the grotesque, "the humorous and the macabre," fade in and out of each other. A good example is the way the word "prefer" creeps into the speech of the other scriveners and into the speech of the Lawyer himself. Bartleby is tragic, in his morbid withdrawal, but "in such grotesque anesthetizations of the self lurks a narcotic charm" and we can see "the hint of something subliminally intimate and wished for in the grotesque."[70]

As we go through the story, we watch with a certain delight how Bartleby is "catching." We root for the spread of the bug. It is something wonderfully wrong in our boring world. Bartleby stands for our instinctive revulsion from all the commands of that world to "behave." Abrams says, "the deepest loyalty of the subconscious is with such a blind, instinctual figure." The Lawyer's opening remarks about how "eminently *safe*" he is are not an unwitting confession; they are the premise of the comic turn. We feel a delicious, subversive joy in the way the man who won't work works wonderfully well. The straight man in this vaudeville routine is the Lawyer, and he keeps coming back, asking the irrational to be reasonable, trying to get the refractory to cooperate. We love to see him defeated, to watch him as he begins "to stagger" and frantically seeks reinforcement for his own "faltering mind."

To whom can he turn? Who can help in his efforts to understand and deal with Bartleby? An awful vacancy opens

70. Robert E. Abrams, "'Bartleby' and the Fragile Pageantry of the Ego," *ELH*, 45 (1978), 488–500, p. 493.

up in his life, the vacancy of his "cool tranquillity" and his "snug retreat." He looks around, and there is nobody there. The emptiness of Bartleby's life seems to tally his own. Where is the friend? The wife? The family? The Lawyer has to consult books, Edwards and Priestly. His own life is a bachelor's. This Lawyer prides himself on his balance—"professionally and privately." He instinctively seeks balance and prides himself on the achievement of it. He deals with the world so that "in a manner, privacy and society were conjoined." But now he is getting all unbalanced, yawing dangerously. It frightens him:

> Presentiments of strange discoveries hovered around me.

> sad fancyings—chimeras, doubtless, of a sick and silly brain

> There was something about Bartleby that not only strangely disarmed me, but in a wonderful manner, touched and disconcerted me.

> I trembled to think that my contact with the scrivener had already and seriously affected me in a mental way. And what further and deeper aberration might it not yet produce?

He is quite explicit about his growing fear that he is losing his mind: "The scrivener's pale form appeared to me laid out, among uncaring strangers, in its shivering winding sheet." Note that wonderful "shivering"—the dead man moves! What we sense here is the amazing susceptibility of this "eminently *safe* man," no longer safe at all, not from Bartleby, and most especially not safe from the haunting voices in his own head. There are, suddenly, deeply frightening voices and images in there. What he thought were brick walls are very slender reeds.

We are inaccurate about the story, and inaccurate about the Lawyer's mind, if we concentrate exclusively on the pathos and the tragedy. We must be able to see, simultaneously, how funny it is. More accurately, we must see a single emotion of great complexity; only in profound doubleness do we apprehend it truly. Weird little pairs of words run through the story, sublime little whimpers "wonderful mildness," "great stillness," "sheer vacancy," "wonderous ascendancy." The mock heroic starts innocently enough in the genial tone of the opening pages, in that touching image of Turkey deploying columns, "myself at their head," gallantly charging the foe, "thus!" with a violent thrust of his ruler. Or Nippers with his desk at the impossibly sharp angle ("like a man using the steep roof of a Dutch house for his desk"). All this works in the little self-conscious details of the Lawyer's speech, as when he mentions "the proprietor of the face." But, as he gets more and more agitated and disoriented, he shouts things like "put up your money" to a voice on the street that says "I'll take odds he doesn't," for it is election day, and "In my intent frame of mind, I had, as it were, imagined that all Broadway shared in my excitement." A man whose chief virtues are "prudence" and "method" literally does not know what he is doing, does not know what he is saying; "If you do not go away from these premises before night, I shall feel bound—indeed I *am* bound—to—to—to quit the premises myself!" That prized balance of mind becomes absurdly demonic self-contradiction. The Lawyer is walking around "with my hand in my pocket—and—and my heart in my mouth," and so "I tore myself from him whom I had so longed to be rid of." The Lawyer is not making sense anymore. The verbal comedy issues into physical comedy: "effectually dodging every one by the suddenness and rapidity of my flight," the Lawyer rushes from the building, and runs "up Wall-street towards Broadway, and jumping into the first omnibus. . . ." The Lawyer is running wild.

Or he is brought abruptly to a halt. When he fumbles at his office door, thinking Bartleby is finally gone, he hears a voice from within—"Not yet; I am occupied," and

> I was thunderstruck. For an instant I stood like the man who, pipe in mouth, was killed one cloudless afternoon long ago in Virginia, by summer lightning; at his own warm open window he was killed, and remained leaning out there upon the dreamy afternoon, till some one touched him, when he fell.

It is a marvelous comic image, elaborately detailed, coming round to that deadpan climax, "when he fell." It follows the funny little admission which peeps up when the Lawyer "stood listening for a moment," and finding that "all was still" assumes Bartleby "must be gone"—and "I was almost sorry for my brilliant success." If the Lawyer stands in for "us," he is doing it here. Like him, we would feel very sorry to find Bartleby gone because we need to see this wonderful game keep going. We do not want Bartleby to shape up. We want him, as long as possible, to go on being Bartleby.

As for our Lawyer, he is a man of fine intelligence, keen wit, and generous humor. But he is helpless when fate drops a lonely young man on his doorstep. All the Lawyer's pride in himself blows up in his face, and his whole life begins to malfunction. That is an interesting story. And the text everywhere supports such a reading.

Look, for example, at this not very important sentence:

> Others may have loftier parts to enact; but my mission in this world, Bartleby, is to furnish you with office-room for such period as you may see fit to remain.

If you see that Lawyer as a dolt, you brush right by it. But if you hear the Lawyer's lovely, resonant voice, it is quite moving. In the very next sentence, the Lawyer turns his back on "this wise and blessed frame of mind." That is the way he works; he is not as strong as he wishes to be. He caves in when "a whisper of wonder was running round, having reference to the strange creature I kept at my office." He says, "This worried me very much." And then he goes a little funny in the head. He wonders if Bartleby might be "a long-lived man." Sane man that he is, the Lawyer begins to dream up a totally fantastic situation in which Bartleby will "keep occupying my chambers, and denying my authority; and perplexing my visitors; and scandalizing my professional reputation; and casting a general gloom over the premises"; and, my God, "in the end perhaps outlive me, and claim possession of my office by right of his perpetual occupancy." Anyone who does not see how funny that is will probably miss, too, that "as all these dark anticipations crowded upon me more and more, and my friends continually intruded their relentless remarks upon the apparition in my room; a great change was wrought in me." He is charged up, resolved "to gather all my faculties together," to swing into action "and for ever rid me of this intolerable incubus." An "incubus" might mean merely one dictionary definition of it, "any person or thing that oppresses or burdens." But here it seems to qualify under the terms of another, darker definition, "an evil spirit, supposed to lie upon persons in their sleep." The narrator is having a real nightmare.

And what does he do? Well, "ere revolving any complicated project, however," our Lawyer sits down to discuss, rationally, with Bartleby, "the propriety of his permanent departure." The Lawyer speaks "in a calm and serious tone," commending his remarks to the "careful and mature consideration" of the incubus himself.

After our Lawyer has "denied" Bartleby three times, and moved away from him into new offices, he is called upon by a "perturbed looking stranger," a lawyer who communicates the problem that Bartleby "refuses to do any thing; he says he prefers not to; and he refuses to quit the premises." We smile at our favorite line tucked in there between semicolons; Bartleby-talk is creeping into the speech of strangers now, too: even though we have moved away from him, he's still Bartleby. The Lawyer tells us, "I found several persons waiting at my door in a high state of nervous excitement." Bartleby's "pallid haughtiness" has turned things upside down: "Every body is concerned; clients are leaving the offices; some fears are entertained of a mob; something you must do, and that without delay." The Lawyer is "aghast at this torrent." And then we get the comic payoff:

> Going up stairs to my old haunt, there was Bartleby silently sitting upon the banister at the landing.
>
> "What are you doing here, Bartleby?" said I.
>
> "Sitting upon the banister," he mildly replied.

Mildly. Bartleby, the crazy man, is keeping his head while all about him are losing theirs. He is the only one who knows what he is doing. He is "sitting upon the banister"—"upon," not "on." When he answers "Sitting upon the banister" to the question "What are you doing here?" we laugh, for we are paying tribute to the pull of the irrational and to the truth lurking in it. Throughout the story Bartleby's replies subvert and contradict the Lawyer's reality. Of course, we want the Lawyer to save Bartleby. But we really want, just as much, for Bartleby to save the Lawyer. We are about equally divided between our desire to have Bartleby come to his senses and our delight in seeing the Lawyer take leave of his.

The Reliable Narrator

In my American Renaissance course it came time for me to teach "Bartleby." Seventy young men and women would be reading it for the first time, and I would have fifty minutes to talk with them about it. I told them I wouldn't give a formal lecture. I told them they would have to write their own "tickets"—one question—and I would try to answer whatever was on the table. I asked them to be simple, to be honest, to say as plainly as they could whatever disturbed or perplexed them when they read it.

On Friday morning I picked up the questions they had placed on the lectern.

Why does Bartleby stop copying?

Why did Bartleby "prefer" to be a scrivener in the first place?

Why does Bartleby stare out the window—is he looking for something?

If the Lawyer is so "safe," why doesn't he throw Bartleby out?

Why does Bartleby copy for three whole days before he stops?

Why does he quit eating?

"Why?"—that's what my students asked—"*Why?*" I answered them as best I could, but at the end of our discussion I quoted to them the verdict of that excellent literary critic, Albert Einstein: "The most beautiful thing we can experience is the mysterious."

In her "In Brief" column at the front of the *New Yorker*, Pauline Kael once in a while mentions the movie

> "Bartleby" (1970)—The shock when you first read the story—Melville's "Bartleby, the Scrivener"—may be in the recognition that Melville had this prevision of modern alienation back in 1853. The character is a precursor of Kafka's central figures, of Oblomov, of Dostoevski's underground man, of Camus's

> Meursault, and you can't grasp how this specifically modern man was formed in that mid-nineteenth-century setting. What is he doing in that world, passively resisting, and withdrawing into courteous, stubborn catatonia?

She is probably right that setting it in modern London "kills the visionary quality right off the bat. . . . The movie was obviously made on a shoestring and with honorable intentions, yet it's tentative and lame; it has little to recommend it but the two actors, Melville's dialogue, and the remnants of his great spooky conception." Kael's phrase "great spooky conception" locates accurately the essential effect of "Bartleby, The Scrivener." It is what I mean by calling the story genuinely haunting. And perhaps we should take that haunting very literally. Bartleby annoys the other characters, and sometimes he provokes them to fury, but he does not haunt them. Bartleby haunts only the narrator. Ghosts do not waste their time on people who cannot see them; ghosts haunt only the people who deserve them. To feel the force of Bartleby's line "I prefer not to," one must hear, in the little silence that follows it, how the line delivers two contradictory meanings, obstinacy and politeness. What makes the line so funny, and so eerie, is the way it stuns the Lawyer every time. He hears its profoundly mixed message, its perfect yes and no. Bartleby's *prefer* creeps insidiously into the speech of his co-workers, and we see it pop up in the messenger from the new tenants of the old office. But only the Lawyer understands, because he can't, quite. He gets used to it, and he does not; he goes on shaking his head in disbelief and nodding it in assent. Bartleby drives the Lawyer out of his mind, for the Lawyer feels as if Bartleby is saying, "I'm what you've got coming to you."

We have to understand the Lawyer's voice because we

derive Bartleby through the Lawyer and only through him. Misunderstand the Lawyer, and you can't understand Bartleby. The truly remarkable thing about our narrator is just how reliable he really is. To say Bartleby "respectfully," "slowly," and "mildly" disappears is to express the profoundest meaning of the story—to understand not the motive of Bartleby's silence but the dimension of it. Especially that "mildly" affords an oceanic calm. The Lawyer plumbs for us the depth of the surface; he can hear that "Sitting upon the banister" and "I prefer not to" partake respectfully, slowly, and mildly of the awesome silence they lead into. They depend on the Lawyer's being there to hear and complete them. Everybody else hears only what Bartleby says; the Lawyer hears the silence in it. Calling the narrator unreliable is really the same mistake as digging beneath the surface to "explain" Bartleby. We substitute little false meanings for the big true one.

On the last page the narrator is still trying to hear something in the silence that "passively resists" all his efforts to comprehend it. Finally he cries, "Ah Bartleby! Ah humanity!" and falls silent himself. In that concluding act of perfectly responsive audition, the Lawyer is a different man from the one who boasted about his "prudence" and "method" at the beginning. He has had to go through an intense personal loss, a family loss. This is a religious emotion, and it comes from the deepest regions of Melville's heart. Bruce Franklin points to it when he cites the Book of Matthew and connects "this forlornest of mankind" to "the least of these." The traditional religious invitation to "give yourself to Christ" is also a command to "Let the Lord into your life." William James said that all religions must begin with an answer to the single cry for help. Bartleby is the cry *Help* incarnate, or so the Lawyer hears it. In the opening paragraphs of the story the Lawyer brags about what we see as wrong with him. At the end he sees it himself. Bartleby came into his life when his life was not much worth living. When Bartleby dies, "I cannot adequately express the emotions which seize me." Grief awakens the man to his own life, and "humanity" is forever changed.

The story is reproduced here with the original punctuation, as it appeared in *Putnam's Monthly Magazine*, November and December, 1853, and without the three lines of by-play about Mrs. Cutlets which Melville excised when he included the story in *The Piazza Tales*, 1856.

Bartleby, The Scrivener

A Story of Wall-street

I am a rather elderly man. The nature of my avocations for the last thirty years has brought me into more than ordinary contact with what would seem an interesting and somewhat singular set of men of whom as yet nothing that I know of has ever been written:—I mean the law-copyists or scriveners. I have known very many of them, professionally and privately, and if I pleased, could relate divers histories, at which good-natured gentlemen might smile, and sentimental souls might weep. But I waive the biographies of all other scriveners for a few passages in the life of Bartleby, who was a scrivener the strangest I ever saw or heard of. While of other law-copyists I might write the complete life, of Bartleby nothing of that sort can be done. I believe that no materials exist for a full and satisfactory biography of this man. It is an irreparable loss to literature. Bartleby was one of those beings of whom nothing is ascertainable, except from the original sources, and in his case those are very small. What my own astonished eyes saw of Bartleby, *that* is all I know of him, except, indeed, one vague report which will appear in the sequel.

Ere introducing the scrivener, as he first appeared to me, it is fit I make some mention of myself, my *employées*, my business, my chambers, and general surroundings; because some such description is indispensable to an adequate understanding of the chief character about to be presented.

Imprimis: I am a man who, from his youth upwards, has been filled with a profound conviction that the easiest way of life is the best. Hence, though I belong to a profession proverbially energetic and nervous, even to turbulence, at times, yet nothing of that sort have I ever suffered to invade my peace. I am one of those unambitious lawyers who never addresses a jury, or in any way draws down public applause; but in the cool tranquillity of a snug retreat, do a snug business among rich men's bonds and mortgages and title-deeds. All who know me, consider me an eminently *safe* man. The late John Jacob Astor, a personage little given to poetic enthusiasm, had no hesitation in pronouncing my first grand point to be prudence; my next, method. I do not speak it in vanity, but simply record the fact, that I was not unemployed in my profession by the late John Jacob Astor; a name which, I admit, I love to repeat, for it hath a rounded and orbicular sound to it, and rings like unto bullion. I will freely add, that I was not insensible to the late John Jacob Astor's good opinion.

Some time prior to the period at which this little history begins, my avocations had been largely increased. The good old office, now extinct in the State of New York, of a Master in Chancery, had been conferred upon me. It was not a very arduous office, but very pleasantly remunerative. I seldom lose my temper; much more seldom indulge in dangerous indignation at wrongs and outrages; but I must be permitted to be rash here and declare, that I consider the sudden and violent abrogation of the office of Master in Chancery, by the new Constitution, as a——premature act; inasmuch as I had counted upon a life-lease of the profits, whereas I only received those of a few short years. But this is by the way.

My chambers were up stairs at No.—Wall-street. At one end they looked upon the white wall of the interior of a spacious sky-light shaft, penetrating the building from top to bottom. This view might have been considered rather tame than otherwise, deficient in what landscape painters call "life." But if so, the view from the other end of my chambers offered, at least, a contrast, if nothing more. In that direction my windows commanded an unobstructed view of a lofty brick wall, black by age and everlasting shade; which wall required no spy-glass to bring out its lurking beauties, but for the benefit of all near-sighted spectators, was pushed up to within ten feet of my window panes. Owing to the great height of the surrounding buildings, and my chambers being on the second floor, the interval between this wall and mine not a little resembled a huge square cistern.

At the period just preceding the advent of Bartleby, I had two persons as copyists in my employment, and a promising lad as an office-boy. First, Turkey; second, Nippers; third, Ginger Nut. These may seem names, the like of which are not usually found in the Directory. In truth they were nick-names, mutually conferred upon each other by my three clerks, and were deemed expressive of their respective persons or characters. Turkey was a short, pursy Englishman of about my own age, that is, somewhere not far from sixty. In the morning, one might say, his face was of a fine florid hue, but after twelve o'clock, meridian—his dinner hour—it blazed like a grate full of Christmas coals; and continued blazing—but, as it were, with a gradual wane—till 6 o'clock, P.M. or thereabouts, after which I saw no more of the proprietor of the face, which gaining its meridian with the sun, seemed to set with it, to rise, culminate, and decline the following day, with the like regularity and undiminished glory. There are many singular coincidences I have known in the course of my life, not the least among which was the fact that exactly when Turkey displayed his fullest beams from his red and radiant countenance, just then, too, at the critical moment, began the daily period when I considered his business capacities as seriously disturbed for the remainder of the twenty-four hours. Not that he was absolutely idle, or averse to business then; far from it. The difficulty was, he was apt to be altogether too energetic. There was a strange, inflamed, flurried, flighty recklessness of activity about him. He would be incautious in dipping his pen into his inkstand. All his blots upon my documents, were dropped there after twelve o'clock, meridian. Indeed, not only would he be reckless and sadly given to making blots in the afternoon, but some days he went further, and was rather noisy. At such times, too, his face flamed with augmented blazonry, as if cannel coal had been heaped on anthracite. He made an unpleasant racket with his chair; spilled his sand-box; in mending his pens, impatiently split them all to pieces, and threw them on the floor in a sudden passion; stood up and leaned over his table, boxing his papers about in a most indecorous manner, very sad to behold in an elderly man like him. Nevertheless, as he was in many ways a most valuable person to me, and all the time before twelve o'clock, meridian, was the quickest, steadiest creature too, accomplishing a great deal of work in a style not easy to be matched—for these reasons, I was willing to overlook his eccentricities, though indeed, occasionally, I remonstrated with him. I did this very gently, however, because, though the civilest, nay, the blandest and most reverential of men in the morning, yet in the afternoon he was disposed, upon provocation, to be slightly rash with his tongue, in fact, insolent. Now, valuing his morning services as I did, and resolved not to lose them; yet, at the same time made uncomfortable by his inflamed ways after twelve o'clock; and being a man of peace, unwilling by my admonitions to call forth unseemingly retorts from him; I took upon me, one Saturday noon (he was always worse on Saturdays), to hint to him, very kindly, that perhaps now that he was growing old, it might be well to abridge his labors; in short, he need not come to my chambers after twelve o'clock, but, dinner over, had best go home to his lodgings and rest himself till tea-time. But no; he insisted upon his afternoon devotions. His countenance became intolerably fervid, as he oratorically assured me—gesticulating with a long ruler at the other end of the room—that if his services in the morning were useful, how indispensable, then, in the afternoon?

"With submission, sir," said Turkey on this occasion, "I consider myself your right-hand man. In the morning I but marshal and deploy my columns; but in the afternoon I put myself at their head, and gallantly charge the foe, thus!"—and he made a violent thrust with the ruler.

"But the blots, Turkey," intimated I.

"True,—but, with submission, sir, behold these hairs! I am getting old. Surely, sir, a blot or two of a warm afternoon is not to be severely urged against gray hairs. Old age—even if it blot the page—is honorable. With submission, sir, we *both* are getting old."

This appeal to my fellow-feeling was hardly to be resisted.

At all events, I saw that go he would not. So I made up my mind to let him stay, resolving, nevertheless, to see to it, that during the afternoon he had to do with my less important papers.

Nippers, the second on my list, was a whiskered, sallow, and, upon the whole, rather piratical-looking young man of about five and twenty. I always deemed him the victim of two evil powers—ambition and indigestion. The ambition was evinced by a certain impatience of the duties of a mere copyist, an unwarrantable usurpation of strictly professional affairs, such as the original drawing up of legal documents. The indigestion seemed betokened in an occasional nervous testiness and grinning irritability, causing the teeth to audibly grind together over mistakes committed in copying; unnecessary maledictions, hissed, rather than spoken, in the heat of business; and especially by a continual discontent with the height of the table where he worked. Though of a very ingenious mechanical turn, Nippers could never get this table to suit him. He put chips under it, blocks of various sorts, bits of pasteboard, and at last went so far as to attempt an exquisite adjustment by final pieces of folded blotting-paper. But no invention would answer. If, for the sake of easing his back, he brought the table lid at a sharp angle well up towards his chin, and wrote there like a man using the steep roof of a Dutch house for his desk:—then he declared that it stopped the circulation in his arms. If now he lowered the table to his waistbands, and stooped over it in writing, then there was a sore aching in his back. In short, the truth of the matter was, Nippers knew not what he wanted. Or, if he wanted anything, it was to be rid of a scrivener's table altogether. Among the manifestations of his diseased ambition was a fondness he had for receiving visits from certain ambiguous-looking fellows in seedy coats, whom he called his clients. Indeed I was aware that not only was he, at times, considerable of a ward-politician, but he occasionally did a little business at the Justices' courts, and was not unknown on the steps of the Tombs. I have good reason to believe, however, that one individual who called upon him at my chambers, and who, with a grand air, he insisted was his client, was no other than a dun, and the alleged title-deed, a bill. But with all his failings, and the annoyances he caused me, Nippers, like his compatriot Turkey, was a very useful man to me; wrote a neat, swift hand; and, when he chose, was not deficient in a gentlemanly sort of deportment. Added to this, he always dressed in a gentlemanly sort of way; and so, incidentally, reflected credit upon my chambers. Whereas with respect to Turkey, I had much ado to keep him from being a reproach to me. His clothes were apt to look oily and smell of eating-houses. He wore his pantaloons very loose and baggy in summer. His coats were execrable; his hat not to be handled. But while the hat was a thing of indifference to me, inasmuch as his natural civility and deference, as a dependent Englishman, always led him to doff it the moment he entered the room, yet his coat was another matter. Concerning his coats, I reasoned with him; but with no effect. The truth was, I suppose, that a man with so small an income, could not afford to sport such a lustrous face and a lustrous coat at one and the same time. As Nippers once observed, Turkey's money went chiefly for red ink. One winter day I presented Turkey with a highly-respectable looking coat of my own, a padded gray coat, of a most comfortable warmth, and which buttoned straight up from the knee to the neck. I thought Turkey would appreciate the favor, and abate his rashness and obstreperousness of afternoons. But no. I verily believe that buttoning himself up in so downy and blanket-like a coat had a pernicious effect upon him; upon the same principle that too much oats are bad for horses. In fact, precisely as a rash, restive horse is said to feel his oats, so Turkey felt his coat. It made him insolent. He was a man whom prosperity harmed.

Though concerning the self-indulgent habits of Turkey I had my own private surmises, yet touching Nippers I was well persuaded that whatever might be his faults in other respects, he was, at least, a temperate young man. But indeed, nature herself seemed to have been his vintner, and at his birth charged him so thoroughly with an irritable, brandy-like disposition, that all subsequent potations were needless. When I consider how, amid the stillness of my chambers, Nippers would sometimes impatiently rise from his seat, and stooping over his table, spread his arms wide apart, seize the whole desk, and move it, and jerk it, with a grim, grinding motion on the floor, as if the table were a perverse voluntary agent, intent on thwarting and vexing him; I plainly perceive that for Nippers, brandy and water were altogether superfluous.

It was fortunate for me that, owing to its peculiar cause—indigestion—the irritability and consequent nervousness of Nippers, were mainly observable in the morning, while in the afternoon he was comparatively mild. So that Turkey's paroxysms only coming on about twelve o'clock, I never had to do with their eccentricities at one time. Their fits relieved each other like guards. When Nippers' was on, Turkey's was off; and *vice versa.* This was a good natural arrangement under the circumstances.

Ginger Nut, the third on my list, was a lad some twelve years old. His father was a carman, ambitious of seeing his son on the bench instead of a cart, before he died. So he sent him to my office as student at law, errand boy, and cleaner and sweeper, at the rate of one dollar a week. He had a little desk to himself, but he did not use it much. Upon inspection, the drawer exhibited a great array of the shells of various sorts of nuts. Indeed, to this quick-witted youth the whole noble science of the law was contained in a nut-shell. Not the least among the employments of Ginger Nut, as well as one which he discharged with the most alacrity, was his duty as cake and apple purveyor for Turkey and Nippers. Copying law papers being proverbially a dry, husky sort of business, my two scriveners were fain to moisten their mouths very often with Spitzenbergs to be had at the numerous stalls nigh the Custom House and Post Office. Also, they sent Ginger Nut very frequently for that peculiar cake—small, flat, round, and very spicy—after which he had been named by them. Of a cold morning when business was but dull, Turkey would gobble up scores of these cakes, as if they were mere wafers—indeed they sell them at the rate of six or eight for a penny—the scrape of his pen blending with the crunching of the crisp particles in his mouth. Of all the fiery afternoon blunders and flurried rashnesses of Turkey, was his once moistening a ginger-cake between his lips, and clapping it on to a mortgage for a seal. I came within an ace of dismissing him then. But he mollified me by making an oriental bow, and saying—"With submission, sir, it was generous of me to find you in stationery on my own account."

Now my original business—that of a conveyancer and title hunter, and drawer-up of recondite documents of all sorts—was considerably increased by receiving the master's office. There was now great work for scriveners. Not only must I push the clerks already with me, but I must have additional help. In answer to my advertisement, a motionless young man one morning, stood upon my office threshold, the door being open, for it was summer. I can see that figure now—pallidly neat, pitiably respectable, incurably forlorn! It was Bartleby.

After a few words touching his qualifications, I engaged him, glad to have among my corps of copyists a man of so singularly sedate an aspect, which I thought might operate beneficially upon the flighty temper of Turkey, and the fiery one of Nippers.

I should have stated before that ground glass folding-doors divided my premises into two parts, one of which was occupied by my scriveners, the other by myself. According to my humor I threw open these doors, or closed them. I resolved to assign Bartleby a corner by the folding-doors, but on my side of them, so as to have this quiet man within easy call, in case any trifling thing was to be done. I placed his desk close up to a small sidewindow in that part of the room, a window which originally had afforded a lateral view of certain grimy back-yards and bricks, but which, owing to subsequent erections, commanded at present no view at all, though it gave some light. Within three feet of the panes was a wall, and the light came down from far above, between two lofty buildings, as from a very small opening in a dome. Still further to a satisfactory arrangement, I procured a high green folding screen, which might entirely isolate Bartleby from my sight, though not remove him from my voice. And thus, in a manner, privacy and society were conjoined.

At first Bartleby did an extraordinary quantity of writing. As if long famishing for something to copy, he seemed to gorge himself on my documents. There was no pause for digestion. He ran a day and night line, copying by sun-light and by candle-light. I should have been quite delighted with his application, had he been cheerfully industrious. But he wrote on silently, palely, mechanically.

It is, of course, an indispensable part of a scrivener's

business to verify the accuracy of his copy, word by word. Where there are two or more scriveners in an office, they assist each other in this examination, one reading from the copy, the other holding the original. It is a very dull, wearisome, and lethargic affair. I can readily imagine that to some sanguine temperaments it would be altogether intolerable. For example, I cannot credit that the mettlesome poet Byron would have contentedly sat down with Bartleby to examine a law document of, say five hundred pages, closely written in a crimpy hand.

Now and then, in the haste of business, it had been my habit to assist in comparing some brief document myself, calling Turkey or Nippers for this purpose. One object I had in placing Bartleby so handy to me behind the screen, was to avail myself of his services on such trivial occasions. It was on the third day, I think, of his being with me, and before any necessity had arisen for having his own writing examined, that, being much hurried to complete a small affair I had in hand, I abruptly called to Bartleby. In my haste and natural expectancy of instant compliance, I sat with my head bent over the original on my desk, and my right hand sideways, and somewhat nervously extended with the copy, so that immediately upon emerging from his retreat, Bartleby might snatch it and proceed to business without the least delay.

In this very attitude did I sit when I called to him, rapidly stating what it was I wanted him to do—namely, to examine a small paper with me. Imagine my surprise, nay, my consternation, when without moving from his privacy, Bartleby in a singularly mild, firm voice, replied, "I would prefer not to."

I sat awhile in perfect silence, rallying my stunned faculties. Immediately it occurred to me that my ears had deceived me, or Bartleby had entirely misunderstood my meaning. I repeated my request in the clearest tone I could assume. But in quite as clear a one came the previous reply, "I would prefer not to."

"Prefer not to," echoed I, rising in high excitement, and crossing the room with a stride, "What do you mean? Are you moon-struck? I want you to help me compare this sheet here—take it," and I thrust it towards him.

"I would prefer not to," said he.

I looked at him steadfastly. His face was leanly composed; his gray eye dimly calm. Not a wrinkle of agitation rippled him. Had there been the least uneasiness, anger, impatience or impertinence in his manner; in other words, had there been any thing ordinarily human about him, doubtless I should have violently dismissed him from the premises. But as it was, I should have as soon thought of turning my pale plaster-of-paris bust of Cicero out of doors. I stood gazing at him awhile, as he went on with his own writing, and then reseated myself at my desk. This is very strange, thought I. What had one best do? But my business hurried me. I concluded to forget the matter for the present, reserving it for my future leisure. So calling Nippers from the other room, the paper was speedily examined.

A few days after this, Bartleby concluded four lengthy documents, being quadruplicates of a week's testimony taken before me in my High Court of Chancery. It became necessary to examine them. It was an important suit, and great accuracy was imperative. Having all things arranged I called Turkey, Nippers and Ginger Nut from the next room, meaning to place the four copies in the hands of my four clerks, while I should read from the original. Accordingly Turkey, Nippers and Ginger Nut had taken their seats in a row, each with his document in hand, when I called to Bartleby to join this interesting group.

"Bartleby! quick, I am waiting."

I heard a slow scrape of his chair legs on the unscraped floor, and soon he appeared standing at the entrance of his hermitage.

"What is wanted?" said he mildly.

"The copies, the copies," said I hurriedly. "We are going to examine them. There"—and I held towards him the fourth quadruplicate.

"I would prefer not to," he said, and gently disappeared behind the screen.

For a few moments I was turned into a pillar of salt, standing at the head of my seated column of clerks. Recovering myself, I advanced towards the screen, and demanded the reason for such extraordinary conduct.

"*Why* do you refuse?"

"I would prefer not to."

With any other man I should have flown outright into a dreadful passion, scorned all further words, and thrust him ignominiously from my presence. But there was something about Bartleby that not only strangely disarmed me, but in a wonderful manner touched and disconcerted me. I began to reason with him.

"These are your own copies we are about to examine. It is labor saving to you, because one examination will answer for your four papers. It is common usage. Every copyist is bound to help examine his copy. Is it not so? Will you not speak? Answer!"

"I prefer not to," he replied in a flute-like tone. It seemed to me that while I had been addressing him, he carefully revolved every statement that I made; fully comprehended the meaning; could not gainsay the irresistible conclusion; but, at the same time, some paramount consideration prevailed with him to reply as he did.

"You are decided, then, not to comply with my request—

a request made according to common usage and common sense?"

He briefly gave me to understand that on that point my judgment was sound. Yes: his decision was irreversible.

It is not seldom the case that when a man is browbeaten in some unprecedented and violently unreasonable way, he begins to stagger in his own plainest faith. He begins, as it were, vaguely to surmise that, wonderful as it may be, all the justice and all the reason is on the other side. Accordingly, if any disinterested persons are present, he turns to them for some reinforcement for his own faltering mind.

"Turkey," said I, "what do you think of this? Am I not right?"

"With submission, sir," said Turkey, with his blandest tone, "I think that you are."

"Nippers," said I, "what do *you* think of it?"

"I think I should kick him out of the office."

(The reader of nice perceptions will here perceive that, it being morning, Turkey's answer is couched in polite and tranquil terms, but Nippers replies in ill-tempered ones. Or, to repeat a previous sentence, Nippers's ugly mood was on duty, and Turkey's off.)

"Ginger Nut," said I, willing to enlist the smallest suffrage in my behalf, "what do *you* think of it?"

"I think, sir, he's a little *luny*," replied Ginger Nut, with a grin.

"You hear what they say," said I, turning towards the screen, "come forth and do your duty."

But he vouchsafed no reply. I pondered a moment in sore perplexity. But once more business hurried me. I determined again to postpone the consideration of this dilemma to my future leisure. With a little trouble we made out to examine the papers without Bartleby, though at every page or two, Turkey deferentially dropped his opinion that this proceeding was quite out of the common; while Nippers, twitching in his chair with a dyspeptic nervousness, ground out between his set teeth occasional hissing maledictions against the stubborn oaf behind the screen. And for his (Nippers's) part, this was the first and the last time he would do another man's business without pay.

Meanwhile Bartleby sat in his hermitage, oblivious to every thing but his own peculiar business there.

Some days passed, the scrivener being employed upon another lengthy work. His late remarkable conduct led me to regard his way narrowly. I observed that he never went to dinner; indeed that he never went any where. As yet I had never of my personal knowledge known him to be outside of my office. He was a perpetual sentry in the corner. At about eleven o'clock though, in the morning, I noticed that Ginger Nut would advance toward the opening in Bartleby's screen, as if silently beckoned thither by a gesture invisible to me where I sat. That boy would then leave the office jingling a few pence, and reappear with a handful of ginger-nuts which he delivered in the hermitage, receiving two of the cakes for his trouble.

He lives, then, on ginger-nuts, thought I; never eats a dinner, properly speaking; he must be a vegetarian then, but no; he never eats even vegetables, he eats nothing but ginger-nuts. My mind then ran on in reveries concerning the probable effects upon the human constitution of living entirely on ginger-nuts. Ginger-nuts are so called because they contain ginger as one of their peculiar constituents, and the final flavoring one. Now what was ginger? A hot, spicy thing. Was Bartleby hot and spicy? Not at all. Ginger, then, had no effect upon Bartleby. Probably he preferred it should have none.

Nothing so aggravates an earnest person as a passive resistance. If the individual so resisted be of a not inhumane temper, and the resisting one perfectly harmless in his passivity; then, in the better moods of the former, he will endeavor charitably to construe to his imagination what proves impossible to be solved by his judgment. Even so, for the most part, I regarded Bartleby and his ways. Poor fellow! thought I, he means no mischief; it is plain he intends no insolence; his aspect sufficiently evinces that his eccentricities are involuntary. He is useful to me. I can get along with him. If I turn him away, the chances are he will fall in with some less indulgent employer, and then he will be rudely treated, and perhaps driven forth miserably to starve. Yes. Here I can cheaply purchase a delicious self-approval. To befriend Bartleby; to humor him in his strange wilfulness, will cost me little or nothing, while I lay up in my soul what will eventually prove a sweet morsel for my conscience. But this mood was not invariable with me. The passiveness of Bartleby sometimes irritated me. I felt strangely goaded on to encounter him in new opposition, to elicit some angry spark from him answerable to my own. But indeed I might as well have essayed to strike fire with my knuckles against a bit of Windsor soap. But one afternoon the evil impulse in me mastered me, and the following little scene ensued:

"Bartleby," said I, "when those papers are all copied, I will compare them with you."

"I would prefer not to."

"How? Surely you do not mean to persist in that mulish vagary?"

No answer.

I threw open the folding-doors near by, and turning upon Turkey and Nippers, exclaimed in an excited manner—

"He says, a second time, he won't examine his papers. What do you think of it, Turkey?"

It was afternoon, be it remembered. Turkey sat glowing like a brass boiler, his bald head steaming, his hands reeling among his blotted papers.

"Think of it?" roared Turkey; "I think I'll just step behind his screen, and black his eyes for him!"

So saying, Turkey rose to his feet and threw his arms into a pugilistic position. He was hurrying away to make good his promise, when I detained him, alarmed at the effect of incautiously rousing Turkey's combativeness after dinner.

"Sit down, Turkey," said I, "and hear what Nippers has to say. What to do you think of it, Nippers? Would I not be justified in immediately dimissing Bartleby?"

"Excuse me, that is for you to decide, sir. I think his conduct quite unusual, and indeed unjust, as regards Turkey and myself. But it may only be a passing whim."

"Ah," exclaimed I, "you have strangely changed your mind then—you speak very gently of him now."

"All beer," cried Turkey; "gentleness is effects of beer—Nippers and I dined together to-day. You see how gentle *I* am, sir. Shall I go and black his eyes?"

"You refer to Bartleby, I suppose. No, not to-day, Turkey," I replied; "pray, put up your fists."

I closed the doors, and again advanced towards Bartleby. I felt additional incentives tempting me to my fate. I burned to be rebelled against again. I remembered that Bartleby never left the office.

"Bartleby," said I, "Ginger Nut is away; just step round to the Post Office, won't you? (it was but a three minutes walk,) and see if there is any thing for me."

"I would prefer not to."

"You *will* not?"

"I *prefer* not."

I staggered to my desk, and sat there in a deep study. My blind inveteracy returned. Was there any other thing in which I could procure myself to be ignominiously repulsed by this lean, penniless wight?—my hired clerk? What added thing is there, perfectly reasonable, that he will be sure to refuse to do?

"Bartleby!"

No answer.

"Bartleby," in a louder tone.

No answer.

"Bartleby," I roared.

Like a very ghost, agreeably to the laws of magical invocation, at the third summons, he appeared at the entrance of his hermitage.

"Go to the next room, and tell Nippers to come to me."

"I prefer not to," he respectfully and slowly said, and mildly disappeared.

"Very good, Bartleby," said I, in a quiet sort of serenely severe self-possessed tone, intimating the unalterable purpose of some terrible retribution very close at hand. At the moment I half intended something of the kind. But upon the whole, as it was drawing towards my dinner-hour, I thought it best to put on my hat and walk home for the day, suffering much from perplexity and distress of mind.

Shall I acknowledge it? The conclusion of this whole business was, that it soon became a fixed fact of my chambers, that a pale young scrivener, by the name of Bartleby, had a desk there; that he copied for me at the usual rate of four cents a folio (one hundred words); but he was permanently exempt from examining the work done by him, that duty being transferred to Turkey and Nippers, one of compliment doubtless to their superior acuteness; moreover, said

Bartleby was never on any account to be dispatched on the most trivial errand of any sort; and that even if entreated to take upon him such a matter, it was generally understood that he would prefer not to—in other words, that he would refuse point-blank.

As days passed on, I became considerably reconciled to Bartleby. His steadiness, his freedom from all dissipation, his incessant industry (except when he chose to throw himself into a standing revery behind his screen), his great stillness, his unalterableness of demeanor under all circumstances, made him a valuable acquisition. One prime thing was this,—*he was always there;*—first in the morning, continually through the day, and the last at night. I had a singular confidence in his honesty. I felt my most precious papers perfectly safe in his hands. Sometimes to be sure I could not, for the very soul of me, avoid falling into sudden spasmodic passions with him. For it was exceeding difficult to bear in mind all the time those strange peculiarities, privileges, and unheard of exemptions, forming the tacit stipulations on Bartleby's part under which he remained in my office. Now and then, in the eagerness of dispatching pressing business, I would inadvertently summon Bartleby, in a short, rapid tone, to put his finger, say, on the incipient tie of a bit of red tape with which I was about compressing some papers. Of course, from behind the screen the usual answer, "I prefer not to," was sure to come; and then, how could a human creature with the common infirmities of our nature, refrain from bitterly exclaiming upon such perverseness—such unreasonableness. However, every added repulse of this sort which I received only tended to lessen the probability of my repeating the inadvertence.

Here it must be said, that according to the custom of most legal gentlemen occupying chambers in densely-populated law buildings, there were several keys to my door. One was kept by a woman residing in the attic, which person weekly scrubbed and daily swept and dusted my apartments. Another was kept by Turkey for convenience sake. The third I sometimes carried in my own pocket. The fourth I knew not who had.

Now, one Sunday morning I happened to go to Trinity Church, to hear a celebrated preacher, and finding myself rather early on the ground, I thought I would walk round to my chambers for a while. Luckily I had my key with me; but upon applying it to the lock, I found it resisted by something inserted from the inside. Quite surprised, I called out; when to my consternation a key was turned from within; and thrusting his lean visage at me, and holding the door ajar, the apparition of Bartleby appeared, in his shirt sleeves, and otherwise in a strangely tattered dishabille, saying quietly that he was sorry, but he was deeply engaged just then, and—preferred not admitting me at present. In a brief word or two, he moreover added, that perhaps I had better walk round the block two or three times, and by that time he would probably have concluded his affairs.

Now, the utterly unsurmised appearance of Bartleby, tenanting my law-chambers of a Sunday morning, with his cadaverously gentlemanly *nonchalance*, yet withal firm and self-possessed, had such a strange effect upon me, that incontinently I slunk away from my own door, and did as desired. But not without sundry twinges of impotent rebellion against the mild effrontery of this unaccountable scrivener. Indeed, it was his wonderful mildness chiefly, which not only disarmed me, but unmanned me, as it were. For I consider that one, for the time, is a sort of unmanned when he tranquilly permits his hired clerk to dictate to him, and order him away from his own premises. Furthermore, I was full of uneasiness as to what Bartleby could possibly be doing in my office in his shirt sleeves, and in an otherwise dismantled condition of a Sunday morning. Was any thing amiss going on? Nay, that was out of the question. It was not to be thought of for a moment that Bartleby was an immoral person. But what could he be doing there?—copying? Nay again, whatever might be his eccentricities, Bartleby was an eminently decorous person. He would be the last man to sit down to his desk in any state approaching to nudity. Besides, it was Sunday; and there was something about Bartleby that forbade the supposition that he would by any secular occupation violate the proprieties of the day.

Nevertheless, my mind was not pacified; and full of a restless curiosity, at last I returned to the door. Without hindrance I inserted my key, opened it, and entered. Bartleby was not to be seen. I looked round anxiously, peeped behind his screen; but it was very plain that he was gone. Upon more closely examining the place, I surmised that for an indefinite period Bartleby must have ate, dressed, and slept in my office, and that too without plate, mirror, or bed. The cushioned seat of a ricketty old sofa in one corner bore the faint impress of a lean, reclining form. Rolled away under his desk, I found a blanket; under the empty grate, a blacking box and brush; on a chair, a tin basin, with soap and a ragged towel; in a newspaper a few crumbs of ginger-nuts and a morsel of cheese. Yes, thought I, it is evident enough that Bartleby has been making his home here, keeping bachelor's hall all by himself. Immediately then the thought came sweeping across me, What miserable friendlessness and loneliness are here revealed! His poverty is great; but his solitude, how horrible! Think of it. Of a Sunday, Wall-street is deserted as Petra; and every night of every day it is an emptiness. This building too, which of week-days hums with industry and life, at nightfall echoes with sheer vacancy, and all through Sunday is forlorn. And here Bartleby makes his home; sole spectator of a solitude which he has seen all populous—a sort of innocent and transformed Marius brooding among the ruins of Carthage!

For the first time in my life a feeling of overpowering stinging melancholy seized me. Before, I had never experienced aught but a not-unpleasing sadness. The bond of a common humanity now drew me irresistibly to gloom. A fraternal melancholy! For both I and Bartleby were sons of Adam. I remembered the bright silks and sparkling faces I had seen that day in gala trim, swan-like sailing down the Mississippi of Broadway; and I contrasted them with the pallid copyist, and thought to myself, Ah, happiness courts the light, so we deem the world is gay; but misery hides aloof, so we deem that misery there is none. These sad fancyings—chimeras, doubtless, of a sick and silly brain—led on to other and more special thoughts, concerning the eccentricities of Bartleby. Presentiments of strange discoveries hovered round me. The scrivener's pale form appeared to me laid out, among uncaring strangers, in its shivering winding sheet.

Suddenly I was attracted by Bartleby's closed desk, the key in open sight left in the lock.

I mean no mischief, seek the gratification of no heartless curiosity, thought I; besides, the desk is mine, and its contents too, so I will make bold to look within. Every thing was methodically arranged, the papers smoothly placed. The pigeon holes were deep, and removing the files of documents, I groped into their recesses. Presently I felt something there, and dragged it out. It was an old bandanna handkerchief, heavy and knotted. I opened it, and saw it was a savings' bank.

I now recalled all the quiet mysteries which I had noted in the man. I remembered that he never spoke but to answer; that though at intervals he had considerable time to himself, yet I had never seen him reading—no, not even a newspaper; that for long periods he would stand looking out, at his pale window behind the screen, upon the dead brick wall; I was quite sure he never visited any refectory or eating house; while his pale face clearly indicated that he never drank beer like Turkey, or tea and coffee even, like other men; that he never went any where in particular that I could learn; never went out for a walk, unless indeed that was the case at present; that he had declined telling who he was, or whence he came, or whether he had any relatives in the world; that though so thin and pale, he never complained of ill health. And more than all, I remembered a certain unconscious air of pallid—how shall I call it?—of pallid haughtiness, say, or rather an austere reserve about him, which had positively awed me into my tame compliance with his eccentricities, when I had feared to ask him to do the slightest incidental thing for me, even though I might know, from his long-continued motionlessness, that behind his screen he must be standing in one of those dead-wall reveries of his.

Revolving all these things, and coupling them with the recently discovered fact that he made my office his constant abiding place and home, and not forgetful of his morbid moodiness; revolving all these things, a prudential feeling began to steal over me. My first emotions had been those of pure melancholy and sincerest pity; but just in proportion as the forlornness of Bartleby grew and grew to my imagination, did that same melancholy merge into fear, that pity into repulsion. So true it is, and so terrible too, that up to a certain point the thought or sight of misery enlists our best affections; but, in certain special cases, beyond that point it does not. They err who would assert that invariably this is owing to the inherent selfishness of the human heart. It rather proceeds from a certain hopelessness of remedying excessive and organic ill. To a sensitive being, pity is not seldom pain. And when at last it is perceived that such pity cannot lead to effectual succor, common sense bids the soul be rid of it. What I saw that morning persuaded me that the scrivener was the victim of innate and incurable disorder. I might give alms to his body; but his body did not pain him; it was his soul that suffered, and his soul I could not reach.

I did not accomplish the purpose of going to Trinity Church that morning. Somehow, the things I had seen disqualified me for the time from church-going. I walked homeward, thinking what I would do with Bartleby. Finally, I resolved upon this;—I would put certain calm questions to him the next morning, touching his history, &c., and if he declined to answer them openly and unreservedly (and I supposed he would prefer not), then to give him a twenty dollar bill over and above whatever I might owe him, and tell him his services were no longer required; but that if in any other way I could assist him, I would be happy to do so, especially if he desired to return to his native place, wherever that might be, I would willingly help to defray the expenses. Moreover, if after reaching home, he found himself at any time in want of aid, a letter from him would be sure of a reply.

The next morning came.

"Bartleby," said I, gently calling to him behind his screen.

No reply.

"Bartleby," said I, in a still gentler tone, "come here; I am not going to ask you to do any thing you would prefer not to do—I simply wish to speak to you."

Upon this he noiselessly slid into view.

"Will you tell me, Bartleby, where you were born?"

"I would prefer not to."

"Will you tell me *any thing* about yourself?"

"I would prefer not to."

"But what reasonable objection can you have to speak to me? I feel friendly towards you."

He did not look at me while I spoke, but kept his glance fixed upon my bust of Cicero, which as I then sat, was directly behind me, some six inches above my head.

"What is your answer, Bartleby?" said I, after waiting a considerable time for a reply, during which his countenance remained immovable, only there was the faintest conceivable tremor of the white attenuated mouth.

"At present I prefer to give no answer," he said, and retired into his hermitage.

It was rather weak in me I confess, but his manner on this occasion nettled me. Not only did there seem to lurk in it a certain disdain, but his perverseness seemed ungrateful, considering the undeniable good usage and indulgence he had received from me.

Again I sat ruminating what I should do. Mortified as I was at his behavior, and resolved as I had been to dismiss him when I entered my office, nevertheless I strangely felt something superstitious knocking at my heart, and forbidding me to carry out my purpose, and denouncing me for a villain if I dared to breathe one bitter word against this forlornest of mankind. At last, familiarly drawing my chair behind his screen, I sat down and said: "Bartleby, never mind then about revealing your history; but let me entreat you, as a friend, to comply as far as may be with the usages of this office. Say now you will help to examine papers tomorrow or next day: in short, say now that in a day or two you will begin to be a little reasonable:—say so, Bartleby."

"At present I would prefer not to be a little reasonable," was his mildly cadaverous reply.

Just then the folding-doors opened, and Nippers approached. He seemed suffering from an unusually bad night's rest, induced by severer indigestion than common. He overheard those final words of Bartleby.

"*Prefer not*, eh?" gritted Nippers—"I'd *prefer* him, if I were you, sir," addressing me—"I'd *prefer* him; I'd give him preferences, the stubborn mule! What is it, sir, pray, that he *prefers* not to do now?"

Bartleby moved not a limb.

"Mr. Nippers," said I, "I'd prefer that you would withdraw for the present."

Somehow, of late I had got into the way of involuntary using this word "prefer" upon all sorts of not exactly suitable occasions. And I trembled to think that my contact with the scrivener had already and seriously affected me in a mental way. And what further and deeper aberration might it not yet produce? This apprehension had not been without efficacy in determining me to summary means.

As Nippers, looking very sour and sulky, was departing, Turkey blandly and deferentially approached.

"With submission, sir," said he, "yesterday I was thinking about Bartleby here, and I think that if he would but prefer to take a quart of good ale every day, it would do much towards mending him, and enabling him to assist in examining his papers."

"So you have got the word too," said I, slightly excited.

"With submission, what word, sir," asked Turkey, respectfully crowding himself into the contracted space behind the screen, and by so doing, making me jostle the scrivener. "What word, sir?"

"I would prefer to be left alone here," said Bartleby, as if offended at being mobbed in his privacy.

"*That's* the word, Turkey," said I—"*that's* it."

"Oh, *prefer?* oh yes—queer word. I never use it myself. But, sir, as I was saying, if he would but prefer—"

"Turkey," interrupted I, "you will please withdraw."

"Oh certainly, sir, if you prefer that I should."

As he opened the folding-door to retire, Nippers at his desk caught a glimpse of me, and asked whether I would prefer to have a certain paper copied on blue paper or white. He did not in the least roguishly accent the word prefer. It was plain that it involuntarily rolled from his tongue. I thought to myself, surely I must get rid of a demented man, who already has in some degree turned the tongues, if not the heads of myself and clerks. But I thought it prudent not to break the dismission at once.

The next day I noticed that Bartleby did nothing but stand at his window in his dead-wall revery. Upon asking him why he did not write, he said that he had decided upon doing no more writing.

"Why, how now? what next?" exclaimed I, "do no more writing?"

"No more."

"And what is the reason?"

"Do you not see the reason for yourself," he indifferently replied.

I looked steadfastly at him, and perceived that his eyes looked dull and glazed. Instantly it occurred to me, that his unexampled diligence in copying by his dim window for the first few weeks of his stay with me might have temporarily impaired his vision.

I was touched. I said something in condolence with him. I

hinted that of course he did wisely in abstaining from writing for a while; and urged him to embrace that opportunity of taking wholesome exercise in the open air. This, however, he did not do. A few days after this, my other clerks being absent, and being in a great hurry to dispatch certain letters by the mail, I thought that, having nothing else earthly to do, Bartleby would surely be less inflexible than usual, and carry these letters to the post-office. But he blankly declined. So, much to my inconvenience, I went myself.

Still added days went by. Whether Bartleby's eyes improved or not, I could not say. To all appearance, I thought they did. But when I asked him if they did, he vouchsafed no answer. At all events, he would do no copying. At last, in reply to my urgings, he informed me that he had permanently given up copying.

"What!" exclaimed I; "suppose your eyes should get entirely well—better than ever before—would you not copy then?"

"I have given up copying," he answered, and slid aside.

He remained as ever, a fixture in my chamber. Nay—if that were possible—he became still more of a fixture than before. What was to be done? He would do nothing in the office: why should he stay there? In plain fact, he had now become a millstone to me, not only useless as a necklace, but afflictive to bear. Yet I was sorry for him. I speak less than truth when I say that, on his own account, he occasioned me uneasiness. If he would but have named a single relative or friend, I would instantly have written, and urged their taking the poor fellow away to some convenient retreat. But he seemed alone, absolutely alone in the universe. A bit of wreck in the mid Atlantic. At length, necessities connected with my business tyrannized over all other considerations. Decently as I could, I told Bartleby that in six days' time he must unconditionally leave the office. I warned him to take measures, in the interval, for procuring some other abode. I offered to assist him in this endeavor, if he himself would but take the first step towards a removal. "And when you finally quit me, Bartleby," added I, "I shall see that you go not away entirely unprovided. Six days from this hour, remember."

At the expiration of that period, I peeped behind the screen, and lo! Bartleby was there.

I buttoned up my coat, balanced myself; advanced slowly towards him, touched his shoulder, and said, "The time has come; you must quit this place; I am sorry for you; here is money; but you must go."

"I would prefer not," he replied, with his back still towards me.

"You *must*."

He remained silent.

Now I had an unbounded confidence in this man's common honesty. He had frequently restored to me six pences and shillings carelessly dropped upon the floor, for I am apt to be very reckless in such shirt-button affairs. The proceeding then which followed will not be deemed extraordinary.

"Bartleby," said I, "I owe you twelve dollars on account; here are thirty-two; the odd twenty are yours.—Will you take it?" and I handed the bills towards him.

But he made no motion.

"I will leave them here then," putting them under a weight on the table. Then taking my hat and cane and going to the door I tranquilly turned and added—"After you have removed your things from these offices, Bartleby, you will of course lock the door—since every one is now gone for the day but you—and if you please, slip your key underneath the mat, so that I may have it in the morning. I shall not see you again; so good-bye to you. If hereafter in your new place of abode I can be of any service to you, do not fail to advise me by letter. Good-bye, Bartleby, and fare you well."

But he answered not a word; like the last column of some ruined temple, he remained standing mute and solitary in the middle of the otherwise deserted room.

As I walked home in a pensive mood, my vanity got the better of my pity. I could not but highly plume myself on my masterly management in getting rid of Bartleby. Masterly I call it, and such it must appear to any dispassionate thinker. The beauty of my procedure seemed to consist in its perfect quietness. There was no vulgar bullying, no bravado of any sort, no choleric hectoring, and striding to and fro across the apartment, jerking out vehement commands for Bartleby to bundle himself off with his beggarly traps. Nothing of the kind. Without loudly bidding Bartleby depart—as an inferior genius might have done—I *assumed* the ground that depart he must; and upon the assumption built all I had to say. The more I thought over my procedure, the more I was charmed with it. Nevertheless, next morning, upon awakening, I had my doubts,—I had somehow slept off the fumes of vanity. One of the coolest and wisest hours a man has, is just after he awakes in the morning. My procedure seemed as sagacious as ever,—but only in theory. How it would prove in practice—there was the rub. It was truly a beautiful thought to have assumed Bartleby's departure; but, after all, that assumption was simply my own, and none of Bartleby's. The great point was, not whether I had assumed that he would quit me, but whether he would prefer so to do. He was more a man of preferences than assumptions.

After breakfast, I walked down town, arguing the probabilities *pro* and *con*. One moment I thought it would prove a miserable failure, and Bartleby would be found all alive at my office as usual; the next moment it seemed certain that I should see his chair empty. And so I kept veering about. At the corner of Broadway and Canal-street, I saw quite an excited group of people standing in earnest conversation.

"I'll take odds he doesn't," said a voice as I passed.

"Doesn't go?—done!" said I, "put up your money."

I was instinctively putting my hand in my pocket to produce my own, when I remembered that this was an election day. The words I had overheard bore no reference to Bartleby, but to the success or non-success of some candidate for the mayoralty. In my intent frame of mind, I had, as it were, imagined that all Broadway shared in my excitement, and were debating the same question with me. I passed on, very thankful that the uproar of the street screened my momentary absent-mindedness.

As I had intended, I was earlier than usual at my office door. I stood listening for a moment. All was still. He must be gone. I tried the knob. The door was locked. Yes, my procedure had worked to a charm; he indeed must be vanished. Yet a certain melancholy mixed with this: I was almost sorry for my brilliant success. I was fumbling under the door mat for the key, which Bartleby was to have left there for me, when accidentally my knee knocked against a panel, producing a summoning sound, and in response a voice came to me from within—"Not yet; I am occupied."

It was Bartleby.

I was thunderstruck. For an instant I stood like the man who, pipe in mouth, was killed one cloudless afternoon long ago in Virginia, by summer lightning; at his own warm open window he was killed, and remained leaning out there upon the dreamy afternoon, till some one touched him, when he fell.

"Not gone!" I murmured at last. But again obeying that wondrous ascendancy which the inscrutable scrivener had over me, and from which ascendency, for all my chafing, I could not completely escape, I slowly went down stairs and out into the street, and while walking round the block, considered what I should next do in this unheard-of perplexity. Turn the man out by an actual thrusting I could not; to drive him away by calling him hard names would not do; calling in the police was an unpleasant idea; and yet, permit him to enjoy his cadaverous triumph over me,—this too I could not think of. What was to be done? or, if nothing could be done, was there any thing further that I could *assume* in the matter? Yes, as before I had prospectively assumed that Bartleby would depart, so now I might retrospectively assume that departed he was. In the legitimate carrying out of this assumption, I might enter my office in a great hurry, and pretending not to see Bartleby at all, walk straight against him as if he were air. Such a proceeding would in a singular degree have the appearance of a home-thrust. It was hardly possible that Bartleby could withstand such an application of the doctrine of assumptions. But upon second thoughts the success of the plan seemed rather dubious. I resolved to argue the matter over with him again.

"Bartleby," said I, entering the office, with a quietly severe expression, "I am seriously displeased. I am pained, Bartleby. I had thought better of you. I had imagined you of such a gentlemanly organization, that in any delicate dilemma a slight hint would suffice—in short, an assumption. But it appears I am deceived. Why," I added, unaffectedly starting, "you have not even touched that money yet," pointing to it, just where I had left it the evening previous.

He answered nothing.

"Will you, or will you not, quit me?" I now demanded in a sudden passion, advancing close to him.

"I would prefer *not* to quit you," he replied, gently emphasizing the *not*.

"What earthly right have you to stay here? Do you pay any rent? Do you pay my taxes? Or is this property yours?"

He answered nothing.

"Are you ready to go on and write now? Are your eyes recovered? Could you copy a small paper for me this morning? or help examine a few lines? or step round to the post-office? In a word, will you do any thing at all, to give a coloring to your refusal to depart the premises?

He silently retired into his hermitage.

I was now in such a state of nervous resentment that I thought it but prudent to check myself at present from further demonstrations. Bartleby and I were alone. I remembered the tragedy of the unfortunate Adams and the still more unfortunate Colt in the solitary office of the latter; and how poor Colt, being dreadfully incensed by Adams, and imprudently permitting himself to get wildly excited, was at unawares hurried into his fatal act—an act which certainly no man could possibly deplore more than the actor himself. Often it had occurred to me in my ponderings upon the subject, that had that altercation taken place in the public street, or at a private residence, it would not have terminated as it did. It was the circumstance of being alone in a solitary office, up stairs, of a building entirely unhallowed by humanizing domestic associations—an uncarpeted office, doubtless, of a dusty, haggard sort of appearance;—this it must have been, which greatly helped to enhance the irritable desperation of the hapless Colt.

But when this old Adam of resentment rose in me and tempted me concerning Bartleby, I grappled him and threw him. How? Why, simply by recalling the divine injunction: "A new commandment give I unto you, that ye love one another." Yes, this it was that saved me. Aside from higher considerations, charity often operates as a vastly wise and prudent principle—a great safeguard to its possessor. Men have committed murder for jealousy's sake, and anger's sake, and hatred's sake, and selfishness' sake, and spiritual pride's sake; but no man that ever I heard of, ever committed a diabolical murder for sweet charity's sake. Mere self-interest, then, if no better motive can be enlisted, should, especially with high-tempered men, prompt all beings to charity and philanthropy. At any rate, upon the occasion in question, I strove to drown my exasperated feelings towards the scrivener by benevolently construing his conduct. Poor fellow, poor fellow! thought I, he don't mean any thing; and besides, he has seen hard times, and ought to be indulged.

I endeavored also immediately to occupy myself, and at the same time to comfort my despondency. I tried to fancy that in the course of the morning, at such time as might prove agreeable to him, Bartleby, of his own free accord, would emerge from his hermitage, and take up some decided line of march in the direction of the door. But no. Half-past twelve o'clock came; Turkey began to glow in the face, overturn his inkstand, and become generally obstreperous; Nippers abated down into quietude and courtesy; Ginger Nut munched his noon apple; and Bartleby remained standing at his window in one of his profoundest deadwall reveries. Will it be credited? Ought I to acknowledge it? That afternoon I left the office without saying one further word to him.

Some days now passed, during which, at leisure intervals I looked a little into "Edwards on the Will," and "Priestley on Necessity." Under the circumstances, those books induced a salutary feeling. Gradually I slid into the persuasion that these troubles of mine touching the scrivener, had been all predestinated from eternity, and Bartleby was billeted upon me for some mysterious purpose of an all-wise Providence, which it was not for a mere mortal like me to fathom.

Yes, Bartleby, stay there behind your screen, thought I; I shall persecute you no more; you are harmless and noiseless as any of these old chairs; in short, I never feel so private as when I know you are here. At least I see it, I feel it; I penetrate to the predestinated purpose of my life. I am content. Others may have loftier parts to enact; but my mission in this world, Bartleby, is to furnish you with office-room for such period as you may see fit to remain.

I believe that this wise and blessed frame of mind would have continued with me, had it not been for the unsolicited and uncharitable remarks obtruded upon me by my professional friends who visited the rooms. But thus it often is, that the constant friction of illiberal minds wears out at last the best resolves of the more generous. Though to be sure, when I reflected upon it, it was not strange that people entering my office should be struck by the peculiar aspect of the unaccountable Bartleby, and so be tempted to throw out some sinister observations concerning him. Sometimes an attorney having business with me, and calling at my office, and finding no one but the scrivener there, would undertake to obtain some sort of precise information from him touching my whereabouts; but without heeding his idle talk, Bartleby would remain standing immovable in the middle of the room. So after contemplating him in that position for a time, the attorney would depart, no wiser than he came.

Also, when a Reference was going on, and the room full of lawyers and witnesses and business was driving fast; some deeply occupied legal gentleman present, seeing Bartleby wholly unemployed, would request him to run round to his (the legal gentleman's) office and fetch some papers for him. Thereupon, Bartleby would tranquilly decline, and remain idle as before. Then the lawyer would give a great stare, and turn to me. And what could I say? At last I was made aware that all through the circle of my professional acquaintance, a whisper of wonder was running round, having reference to the strange creature I kept at my office. This worried me very much. And as the idea came upon me of his possibly turning out a long-lived man, and keep occupying my chambers, and denying my authority; and perplexing my visitors; and scandalizing my professional reputation; and casting a general gloom over the premises; keeping soul and body together to the last upon his savings (for doubtless he spent but half a dime a day), and in the end perhaps outlive me, and claim possession of my office by right of his perpetual occupancy: as all these dark anticipations crowded upon me more and more, and my friends continually intruded their relentless remarks upon the apparition in my room; a great change was wrought in me. I resolved to gather all my faculties together, and for ever rid me of this intolerable incubus.

Ere revolving any complicated project, however, adapted to this end, I first simply suggested to Bartleby the propriety of his permanent departure. In a calm and serious tone, I commended the idea to his careful and mature consideration. But having taken three days to meditate upon it, he apprised me that his original determination remained the same; in short, that he still preferred to abide with me.

What shall I do? I now said to myself, buttoning up my coat to the last button. What shall I do? what ought I to do? what does conscience say I *should* do with this man, or rather ghost. Rid myself of him, I must; go, he shall. But how? You will not thrust him, the poor, pale, passive mortal,—you will not thrust such a helpless creature out of your door? you will not dishonor yourself by such cruelty? No, I will not, I cannot do that. Rather would I let him live and die here, and then mason up his remains in the wall. What then will you do? For all your coaxing, he will not budge. Bribes he leaves under your own paperweight on your table; in short, it is quite plain that he prefers to cling to you.

Then something severe, something unusual must be done. What! surely you will not have him collared by a constable, and commit his innocent pallor to the common jail? And upon what ground could you procure such a thing to be done?—a vagrant, is he? What! he a vagrant, a wanderer, who refuses to budge? It is because he will *not* be a vagrant, then, that you seek to count him *as* a vagrant. That is too absurd. No visible means of support: there I have him. Wrong again: for indubitably he *does* support himself, and that is the only unanswerable proof that any man can show of his possessing the means so to do. No more then. Since he will not quit me, I must quit him. I will change my offices; I will move elsewhere; and give him fair notice, that if I find him on my new premises I will then proceed against him as a common trespasser.

Acting accordingly, next day I thus addressed him: "I find these chambers too far from the City Hall; the air is unwholesome. In a word, I propose to remove my offices next week, and shall no longer require your services. I tell you this now, in order that you may seek another place."

He made no reply, and nothing more was said.

On the appointed day I engaged carts and men, proceeded to my chambers, and having but little furniture, every thing was removed in a few hours. Throughout, the scrivener remained standing behind the screen, which I directed to be removed the last thing. It was withdrawn; and being folded up like a huge folio, left him the motionless occupant of a naked room. I stood in the entry watching him a moment, while something from within me upbraided me.

I re-entered, with my hand in my pocket—and—and my heart in my mouth.

"Good-bye, Bartleby; I am going—good-bye, and God

some way bless you; and take that," slipping something in his hand. But it dropped upon the floor, and then,—strange to say—I tore myself from him whom I had so longed to be rid of.

Established in my new quarters, for a day or two I kept the door locked, and started at every footfall in the passages. When I returned to my rooms after any little absence, I would pause at the threshold for an instant, and attentively listen, ere applying my key. But these fears were needless. Bartleby never came nigh me.

I thought all was going well, when a perturbed looking stranger visited me, inquiring whether I was the person who had recently occupied rooms at No.—Wall-street.

Full of forebodings, I replied that I was.

"Then sir," said the stranger, who proved a lawyer, "you are responsible for the man you left there. He refuses to do any copying; he refuses to do any thing; he says he prefers not to; and he refuses to quit the premises."

"I am very sorry, sir," said I, with assumed tranquillity, but an inward tremor, "but, really, the man you allude to is nothing to me—he is no relation or apprentice of mine, that you should hold me responsible for him."

"In mercy's name, who is he?"

"I certainly cannot inform you. I know nothing about him. Formerly I employed him as a copyist; but he has done nothing for me now for some time past."

"I shall settle him then,—good morning, sir."

Several days passed, and I heard nothing more; and though I often felt a charitable prompting to call at the place and see poor Bartleby, yet a certain squeamishness of I know not what withheld me.

All is over with him, by this time, thought I at last, when through another week no further intelligence reached me.

But coming to my room the day after, I found several persons waiting at my door in a high state of nervous excitement.

"That's the man—here he comes," cried the foremost one, whom I recognized as the lawyer who had previously called upon me alone.

"You must take him away, sir, at once," cried a portly person among them, advancing upon me, and whom I knew to be the landlord of No.—Wall-street. "These gentlemen, my tenants, cannot stand it any longer; Mr. B—" pointing to the lawyer, "has turned him out of his room, and he now persists in haunting the building generally, sitting upon the banisters of the stairs by day, and sleeping in the entry by night. Every body is concerned; clients are leaving the offices; some fears are entertained of a mob; something you must do, and that without delay."

Aghast at this torrent, I fell back before it, and would fain have locked myself in my new quarters. In vain I persisted that Bartleby was nothing to me—no more than to any one else. In vain:—I was the last person known to have any thing to do with him, and they held me to the terrible account. Fearful then of being exposed in the papers (as one person present obscurely threatened) I considered the matter, and at length said, that if the lawyer would give me a confidential interview with the scrivener, in his (the lawyer's) own room, I would that afternoon strive my best to rid them of the nuisance they complained of.

Going up stairs to my old haunt, there was Bartleby silently sitting upon the banister at the landing.

"What are you doing here, Bartleby?" said I.

"Sitting upon the banister," he mildly replied.

I motioned him into the lawyer's room, who then left us.

"Bartleby," said I, "are you aware that you are the cause of great tribulation to me, by persisting in occupying the entry after being dismissed from the office?"

No answer.

"Now one of two things must take place. Either you must do something or something must be done to you. Now what sort of business would you like to engage in? Would you like to re-engage in copying for some one?"

"No; I would prefer not to make any change."

"Would you like a clerkship in a dry-goods store?"

"There is too much confinement about that. No, I would not like a clerkship; but I am not particular."

"Too much confinement," I cried, "why you keep yourself confined all the time!"

"I would prefer not to take a clerkship," he rejoined, as if to settle that little item at once.

"How would a bar-tender's business suit you? There is no trying of the eyesight in that."

"I would not like it at all; though, as I said before, I am not particular."

His unwonted wordiness inspirited me. I returned to the charge.

"Well then, would you like to travel through the country collecting bills for the merchants? That would improve your health."

"No, I would prefer to be doing something else."

"How then would going as a companion to Europe, to entertain some young gentleman with your conversation,—how would that suit you?"

"Not at all. It does not strike me that there is any thing definite about that. I like to be stationary. But I am not particular."

"Stationary you shall be then," I cried, now losing all patience, and for the first time in all my exasperating connection with him fairly flying into a passion. "If you do not go away from these premises before night, I shall feel bound—indeed I *am* bound—to—to—to quit the premises myself!" I rather absurdly concluded, knowing not with what possible threat to try to frighten his immobility into compliance. Despairing of all further efforts, I was precipitately leaving him, when a final thought occurred to me—one which had not been wholly unindulged before.

"Bartleby," said I, in the kindest tone I could assume under such exciting circumstances, "will you go home with me now—not to my office, but my dwelling—and remain there till we can conclude upon some convenient arrangement for you at our leisure? Come, let us start now, right away."

"No: at present I would prefer not to make any change at all."

I answered nothing; but effectually dodging every one by the suddenness and rapidity of my flight, rushed from the building, ran up Wall-street towards Broadway, and jumping into the first omnibus was soon removed from pursuit. As soon as tranquility returned I distinctly perceived that I had now done all that I possibly could, both in respect to the demands of the landlord and his tenants, and with regard to my own desire and sense of duty, to benefit Bartleby, and shield him from rude persecution. I now strove to be entirely care-free and quiescent; and my conscience justified me in the attempt; though indeed it was not so successful as I could have wished. So fearful was I of being again hunted out by the incensed landlord and his exasperated tenants, that, surrendering my business to Nippers, for a few days I drove about the upper part of the town and through the suburbs, in my rockaway; crossed over to Jersey City and Hoboken, and paid fugitive visits to Manhattanville and Astoria. In fact I almost lived in my rockaway for the time.

When again I entered my office, lo, a note from the landlord lay upon the desk. I opened it with trembling hands. It informed me that the writer had sent to the police, and had Bartleby removed to the Tombs as a vagrant. Moreover, since I knew more about him than any one else, he wished me to appear at that place, and make a suitable statement of the facts. These tidings had a conflicting effect upon me. At first I was indignant; but at last almost approved. The landlord's energetic, summary disposition, had led him to adopt a procedure which I do not think I would have decided upon myself; and yet as a last resort, under such peculiar circumstances, it seemed the only plan.

As I afterwards learned, the poor scrivener, when told that he must be conducted to the Tombs, offered not the slightest obstacle, but in his pale unmoving way, silently acquiesced.

Some of the compassionate and curious bystanders joined the party; and headed by one of the constables arm in arm with Bartleby, the silent procession filed its way through all the noise, and heat, and joy of the roaring thoroughfares at noon.

The same day I received the note I went to the Tombs, or to speak more properly, the Halls of Justice. Seeking the right officer, I stated the purpose of my call, and was informed that the individual I described was indeed within. I then assured the functionary that Bartleby was a perfectly honest man, and greatly to be compassionated, however unaccountably eccentric. I narrated all I knew, and closed by suggesting the idea of letting him remain in as indulgent confinement as possible till something less harsh might be done—though indeed I hardly knew what. At all events, if nothing else could be decided upon, the alms-house must receive him. I then begged to have an interview.

Being under no disgraceful charge, and quite serene and harmless in all his ways, they had permitted him freely to wander about the prison, and especially in the inclosed grass-platted yards thereof. And so I found him there, standing all alone in the quietest of the yards, his face towards a high wall, while all around, from the narrow slits of the jail windows, I thought I saw peering out upon him the eyes of murderers and thieves.

"Bartleby!"

"I know you," he said, without looking round,—"and I want nothing to say to you."

"It was not I that brought you here, Bartleby," said I, keenly pained at his implied suspicion. "And to you, this should not be so vile a place. Nothing reproachful attaches to you by being here. And see, it is not so sad a place as one might think. Look, there is the sky, and here is the grass."

"I know where I am," he replied, but would say nothing more, and so I left him.

As I entered the corridor again, a broad meat-like man, in an apron, accosted me, and jerking his thumb over his shoulder said—"Is that your friend?"

"Yes."

"Does he want to starve? If he does, let him live on the prison fare, that's all."

"Who are you?" asked I, not knowing what to make of such an unofficially speaking person in such a place.

"I am the grub-man. Such gentlemen as have friends here, hire me to provide them with something good to eat."

"Is this so?" said I, turning to the turnkey.

He said it was.

"Well then," said I, slipping some silver into the grubman's hands (for so they called him). "I want you to give particular attention to my friend there; let him have the best dinner you can get. And you must be as polite to him as possible."

"Introduce me, will you?" said the grub-man, looking at

me with an expression which seemed to say he was all impatience for an opportunity to give a specimen of his breeding.

Thinking it would prove of benefit to the scrivener, I acquiesced; and asking the grub-man his name, went up with him to Bartleby.

"Bartleby, this is a friend; you will find him very useful to you."

"Your sarvant, sir, your sarvant," said the grub-man, making a low salutation behind his apron. "Hope you find it pleasant here, sir;—spacious grounds—cool apartments, sir—hope you'll stay with us some time—try to make it agreeable. What will you have for dinner today?"

"I prefer not to dine to-day," said Bartleby, turning away. "It would disagree with me; I am unused to dinners." So saying he slowly moved to the other side of the inclosure, and took up a position fronting the dead-wall.

"How's this?" said the grub-man, addressing me with a stare of astonishment. "He's odd, aint he?"

"I think he is a little deranged," said I, sadly.

"Deranged? deranged is it? Well now, upon my word, I thought that friend of yourn was a gentleman forger; they are always pale and genteel-like, them forgers. I can't help pity 'em—can't help it, sir. Did you know Monroe Edwards?" he added touchingly, and paused. Then, laying his hand pityingly on my shoulder, sighed, "he died of consumption at Sing-Sing. So you weren't acquainted with Monroe?"

"No, I was never socially acquainted with any forgers. But I cannot stop longer. Look to my friend yonder. You will not lose by it. I will see you again."

Some few days after this, I again obtained admission to the Tombs, and went through the corridors in quest of Bartleby; but without finding him.

"I saw him coming from his cell not long ago," said a turnkey, "may be he's gone to loiter in the yards."

So I went in that direction.

"Are you looking for the silent man?" said another turnkey passing me. "Yonder he lies—sleeping in the yard there. 'Tis not twenty minutes since I saw him lie down."

The yard was entirely quiet. It was not accessible to the common prisoners. The surrounding walls, of amazing thickness, kept off all sound behind them. The Egyptian character of the masonry weighed upon me with its gloom. But a soft imprisoned turf grew under foot. The heart of the eternal pyramids, it seemed, wherein, by some strange magic, through the clefts, grass-seed, dropped by birds, had sprung.

Strangely huddled at the base of the wall, his knees drawn up, and lying on his side, his head touching the cold stones, I saw the wasted Bartleby. But nothing stirred. I paused; then went close up to him; stooped over, and saw that his dim eyes were open; otherwise he seemed profoundly sleeping. Something prompted me to touch him. I felt his hand, when a tingling shiver ran up my arm and down my spine to my feet.

The round face of the grub-man peered upon me now. "His dinner is ready. Won't he dine to-day, either? Or does he live without dining?"

"Lives without dining," said I, and closed the eyes.

"Eh!—He's asleep, aint he?"

"With kings and counsellors," murmured I.

* * * * * * * *

There would seem little need for proceeding further in this history. Imagination will readily supply the meagre recital of poor Bartleby's interment. But ere parting with the reader, let me say, that if this little narrative has sufficiently interested him, to awaken curiosity as to who Bartleby was, and what manner of life he led prior to the present narrator's making his acquaintance, I can only reply, that in such curiosity I fully share, but am wholly unable to gratify it. Yet here I hardly know whether I should divulge one little item of rumor, which came to my ear a few months after the scrivener's decease. Upon what basis it rested, I could never ascertain; and hence how true it is I cannot now tell. But inasmuch as this vague report has not been without a certain strange suggestive interest to me, however sad, it may prove the same with some others; and so I will briefly mention it. The report was this: that Bartleby had been a subordinate clerk in the Dead Letter Office at Washington, from which he had been suddenly removed by a change in the administration. When I think over this rumor, I cannot adequately express the emotions which seize me. Dead letters! does it not sound like dead men? Conceive a man by nature and misfortune prone to a pallid hopelessness, can any business seem more fitted to heighten it than that of continually handling these dead letters and assorting them for the flames? For by the cart-load they are annually burned. Sometimes from out the folded paper the pale clerk takes a ring:—the finger it was meant for, perhaps, moulders in the grave; a bank-note sent in swiftest charity:—he whom it would relieve, nor eats nor hungers any more; pardon for those who died despairing; hope for those who died unhoping; good tidings for those who died stifled by unrelieved calamities. On errands of life, these letters speed to death.

Ah Bartleby! Ah humanity!

Index

Index

Index

Index

Index

Library of Congress Cataloging-in-Publication Data

McCall, Dan.
The silence of Bartleby / Dan McCall.
p. cm.
Includes index.
ISBN 0-8014-2320-1 (alk. paper). — ISBN 0-8014-9593-8 (pbk.: alk. paper)
1. Melville, Herman. 1819–1891. Bartleby, the scrivener. I. Title.
PS2384.B28M3 1989 813'.3—dc19 89-627